EXPLORING THE FAITH WE SHARE

EXPLORING THE FAITH WE SHARE

Edited by

Glenn C. Stone

and

Charles LaFontaine, S.A.

PAULIST PRESS
New York / Ramsey

Acknowledgements
Excerpts from *Profiles in Belief* by Arthur Carl Piepkorn are reprinted by
permission of Harper & Row, Publishers. An excerpt from *The Meaning of Sacred
Scripture* by Louis Bouyer, © 1958 by the University of Notre Dame Press, Notre
Dame, Ind. 46556, is reprinted by permission. Material by Richard F. Smith, S.J.
from "Inspiration and Inerrancy" in *The Jerome Biblical Commentary*, Brown,
Fitzmyer, and Murphy eds., © 1968 Vol. II, p. 500, is reprinted by permission of
Prentice-Hall, Inc., Englewood Cliffs, N.J. Excerpts from the English translation of
The Roman Missal, © 1973, is reprinted by permission of the International
Committee on English in the Liturgy, Inc.; all rights reserved. Selections from the
eucharistic prayer in the holy communion are taken from the *Lutheran Book of
Worship*, pew edition, © 1978, by permission of Augsburg Publishing House,
representing the publishers and copyright holders.

Library of Congress
Catalog Card Number: 79-92856

ISBN: 0-8091-2301-0

Published by Paulist Press
Editorial Office: 1865 Broadway, New York, N.Y. 10023
Business Office: 545 Island Road, Ramsey, N.J. 07446

Printed and bound in the
United States of America

Contents

A Note from the Editors

Early in 1978, at an informal meeting in New York City between staff members of the Graymoor Ecumenical Institute and the American Lutheran Publicity Bureau *(Lutheran Forum)*, this book had its humble beginnings. The meeting had been called to discuss possible ways for Roman Catholics and Lutherans to share more widely the bilateral dialogues between the two communions in the United States. The approach of the 450th anniversary of the Augsburg Confession in 1980 offered an especially appropriate occasion for such sharing.

We soon agreed that a "simple study guide" would be very helpful in "translating" the high-powered documents that have emerged from the Lutheran/Roman Catholic conversations into meaningful, comprehensible terms for average persons in both church traditions. After a time, however, it became clear that a "simple study guide" would have to give way to a book—of modest proportions, of course.

Sometime later, a group of writers from both traditions met several times to plan the proposed volume. They decided that, while particular persons would be assigned to write the various chapters, the final product would be the work of the entire group. That process, though complicated, proceeded surprisingly well, and this book is the result of our communal efforts.

It is appropriate to thank the following persons for their participation with us in this cooperative effort by Lutherans and Roman Catholics: Pastor Larry Bailey, Pastor Ronald Bagnall, Father John Calhoun, Father Patrick Granfield, O.S.B., Father Kevin Irwin, Pastor Leonard Klein, Pastor Richard John Neuhaus and Dr. Gail Ramshaw Schmidt. Our appreciation is also extended to Father Avery Dulles, S.J. and Dr. George Lindbeck, who have provided us with the rich benefits of their long experience in the Lutheran/Roman Catholic dialogues in the United States. The editors and staff of Paulist Press have made our editorial task a good deal easier than we have really deserved.

To all who read and use them, we offer these pages in the hope that the day of Lutheran/Roman Catholic reconciliation will thereby be brought closer to realization.

Charles V. LaFontaine, S.A.
Editor, *Ecumenical Trends*

Glenn C. Stone
Editor, *Lutheran Forum*

November 11, 1979
Commemoration of
St. Martin of Tours and
Søren Kierkegaard

Foreword

This book is occasioned by two major developments in the field of Lutheran/Roman Catholic relations. The first is the 450th anniversary of the Augsburg Confession, commemorated on June 25, 1980. Composed by Philip Melanchthon in 1530 for the Diet of Augsburg, that confession was an attempt to state the case for the Lutheran movement in such a way that it could be accepted by all as having a legitimate place within the one, holy, catholic Church. Melanchthon's preface, reproducing the language of the imperial summons, asked both the papal and the Lutheran parties to "put aside whatever may not have been rightly interpreted or treated by either side, to have all of us embrace and adhere to a single, true religion and live together in unity in one fellowship and church, even as we are all enlisted under one Christ."

In the polemically charged atmosphere of the sixteenth century, the Augsburg Confession did not achieve the unity for which it was intended. But recent scholarship, both Lutheran and Catholic, has established that, whether or not Catholic "recognition" is in order, the Confession unquestionably can serve as a means of recovering the rich heritage common to the two traditions and of finding a path toward closer unity. When read and discussed today, from the perspectives of contemporary Lutheran and Catholic theology, it suggests avenues of reconciliation.

Looking forward to the anniversary of the Augsburg Confession, the United States committee of Catholic and Lutheran bishops and church presidents, at its annual meeting in March 1979, urged "Lutherans and Catholics to consider together a confession which sought to provide a base for the continuing unity of the Church," keeping in mind the unitive intent behind the Confession itself.

The second fact occasioning this book is the progress of the Lutheran-Roman Catholic bilateral discussions. The dialogue in the U.S.A., commissioned by the Catholic Bishops' Committee for Ecumenical and Interreligious Affairs and by Lutheran World Ministries (the U.S.A. Committee of the Lutheran World Federation), has been especially prolific. It has published six volumes of consensus statements and background papers: *The Nicene Creed as Dogma* (1965), *One Baptism for the Remission of Sins* (1966), *The Eucharist as Sacrifice* (1968), *Eucharist and Ministry* (1970), *Papal Primacy and the Universal Church* (1974), and *Teaching Authority and Infallibility* (1979). The dialogue has gone on to consider the question of justification, the theme with which the Reformation began.

These statements of the U.S. dialogue, together with those of the International Lutheran-Catholic Joint Commission, have been hailed in many countries as solid, productive, and potentially fruitful. They manifest greater convergence on central theological issues than has emerged in any other discussions between Catholic and Protestant churches.

One reason for the relative success of these conversations is that Lutherans retained more of the medieval Catholic heritage than other Protestant communions (with the exception of the Anglicans who, however, include large groups which do not regard themselves as Protestant). The Lutheran Reformers were in favor of preserving the tradition as it had developed during fifteen hundred years of Christian history except at those points where it had in their view become opposed to the Gospel. They did not try, as did many other Protestants, to disregard the intervening centuries and literally reproduce New Testament patterns of worship and church government (which in any case, as we are now aware through historical-critical work, were highly variegated and often badly misunderstood by those who tried to reinstate them). To this day, therefore, Lutherans are markedly more sacramental, liturgical, and creedal than other Protestants. Justification by faith and the primacy of Scripture are for them principles corrective of historic Catholicism rather than constitutive of a new form of Christianity. Thus in the sixteenth century, they wished to maintain episcopacy (as the Augsburg Confession makes evident) and communion with the Pope (as appears in other confessional writings such as the Appendix to the Smalcald

Articles). Their only condition was that they be allowed what they called "freedom to preach the Gospel." Where the bishops consented to this, as in Scandinavia, they remained in office. In short, the Lutherans initially insisted that they were a reform movement within the Western Church. Their desire, one might say, was to be both Protestant and Catholic, evangelical and ecclesial, Reformed and Roman.

These attitudes, to be sure, did not persist. After the failure of the efforts at Augsburg and elsewhere to maintain unity, Lutherans came increasingly to share the views of other and later forms of Protestantism that the Roman Catholic Church is not a mother to be renewed but an enemy to be destroyed. Yet the reverse position is represented by the Augsburg Confession which remains for all Lutherans their basic and most authoritative doctrinal standard (apart from the ancient creeds which they share with Catholics). As a consequence, Lutherans who become involved in the contemporary ecumenical search for Christian unity have special incentives and opportunities to explore the possibilities of rapprochement with Rome. When they do this, they are not repudiating their past, but are seeking to regain and reaffirm their original Reformation heritage. They are not losing their distinctive communal identity, but are shaping and clarifying it. They are seeking to become in reality what they officially and originally professed to be: a reform movement within the Catholic Church of the West. Much more clearly than other Protestants, Lutherans are mandated by their heritage and their doctrine to strive for unity, not only with all Christians, but also specifically with Roman Catholics. This is one of the factors which helps account for the exceptional progress in the Lutheran/ Roman Catholic dialogue.

It needs also to be observed, however, that the United States has been the leader in this progress. One reason for this is that Lutherans in the U.S. (and Canada) have had to struggle harder than in Europe to preserve the Catholic elements in their heritage. They are not here the great majority of Protestants as in Scandinavia and Germany, but are rather a relatively small minority in a non-Lutheran Protestant culture which in both its conservative evangelical and theologically liberal forms is on the whole much less sacramental, liturgical, and creedal than they are. This has made many North American Lutherans especially appreciative of the Catholic dimension of their heritage, and of their affinities with the Roman Catholic tradition as this is being renewed since the Second Vatican Council. One could even say that denominational self-interest in the form of a desire to maintain Lutheran distinctiveness amid a non-Lutheran Protestant majority has contributed to the relatively greater success of the Lutheran/Roman Catholic dialogue in North America than in Europe or the third world.

For their part, Catholics entered rather late into the ecumenical dialogue which had been actively under way among Orthodox, Anglicans and Protestants for half a century before Vatican II. The predominant stance of the Roman Catholic community since the sixteenth century had been polemical. Many had become accustomed to looking on Luther as the author of the principle of private judgment, which was allegedly responsible for the almost total dissipation of the Christian substance. When, about the time of Vatican II, Catholics did begin to explore the possibilities of accord with other Christians, they were surprised to discover how staunchly Lutherans still adhered to the doctrinal and sacramental heritage of medieval Christianity. Founded by a Catholic priest who was trained as a monk, biblical exegete and theologian, the Lutheran movement provided an ideal dialogue partner for testing whether the disputes of the sixteenth century still had to be a cause of division between the churches. Could the Lutheran critique even help Catholics to renew their own Church in accordance with the mandate of Vatican II?

The cordial relationships which developed among the American participants, including such eminent churchmen as Warren Quanbeck, John Courtney Murray, Arthur Carl Piepkorn, Kent Knutson and Paul Empie—to mention only those now deceased—gave added reason for the leaders of the respective churches to lend generous support to the Lutheran/Roman Catholic dialogue in the United States.

This leadership role, however, means that the North American dialogue has special opportunities and responsibilities. It has already helped stimulate advances in Lutheran/Roman Catholic conversations in Europe and on the world level. It may in addition, however, be crucial for the entire area of Protestant/Roman Catholic relations. Lutherans, however important the Roman Catholic elements in their tradition, are emphatically Protestant. The Reformation started with them. They are committed to the centrality of justification through faith in Jesus Christ for all aspects of individual and communal Christian life. They can and should think of themselves in their relations to the Roman Catholic Church as acting in some sense on behalf of all Protestants. To the degree that they achieve reconciliation between Rome and the Reformation, they may provide models which others can follow in their own ways. Just as the breach between Protestantism and Roman Catholicism started with them, so they have special obligations and possibilities in the attempt to heal it.

The exceptional possibilities for dialogue in the U.S. also place unusual responsibilities on American Roman Catholics. They are the only ones who can know the local situation well enough to be able to respond to its particular imperatives and opportunities. Such responses, however, require openness, flexibility, and the ability to take independent initiatives when necessary. Much courage and prudence are required.

Perhaps the most urgent need at this point in the dialogue is for greater participation of the whole people of God. The dialogue publications have until now been directed primarily to theological audiences and have been taken up with rather technical doctrinal issues debated between the churches since the sixteenth century. Local congregations have still not been adequately informed about the intentions, methods and results of the dialogues. For this reason it is understandable that many Christians in each tradition are hostile, suspicious or at least confused, while others naively surmise that all theological differences have been successfully transcended. Before the results of the dialogue can be translated into practical measures to be implemented in the local churches, the pastors and faithful of both traditions must become involved in Lutheran/Roman Catholic ecumenism on the "grass-roots" level. Thus far, such ecumenism has been achieved in only a few localities.

At a meeting in February 1978, attended by both authors of this Foreword, the staffs of Lutheran Forum and of the Graymoor Ecumenical Institute reflected on the possibilities of future Lutheran/ Roman Catholic relations in the United States. They proposed that the 450th anniversary year of the Augsburg Confession be dedicated to the goal of healing the breach of the sixteenth century, and that special efforts in this direction be conducted beginning with Reformation Sunday, 1979. The year, they suggested, could suitably culminate in the celebration of "Reformation/Reconciliation Sunday" in October 1980.

As one of the principal study aids to be used for this year of ecumenism, the staffs of Lutheran Forum and the Graymoor Ecumenical Institute resolved to commission the present volume, which is a reflection on the published results, thus far, of the Lutheran/Roman Catholic dialogue in the United States.

The authors of the following chapters, carefully selected for their scholarly competence and ecumenical sensitivity, have diligently sought, within the space allotted to them, to give a fair indication of the principal findings of the dialogue. But as experts in theology or pastoral practice, they have also proposed certain insights and suggestions of their own. They write not as mere reporters but as active participants in the ecumenical conversations they describe.

As members of the Lutheran/Roman Catholic dialogue, we are convinced that a careful study of the present symposium, both by individuals and by discussion groups, will prove informative and stimulating. It should help pastors and members of the churches to become more deeply engaged in the movement toward unity which the Holy Spirit is manifestly stirring up in our time. In this way they can help, some centuries later, to bring about the desire of Emperor Charles V and of Philip Melanchthon that Christians of both parties might "live together in unity in one fellowship and Church."

Avery Dulles, S.J.
George Lindbeck

Father Dulles is a Roman Catholic participant in the dialogues sponsored by the U.S.A. National Committee of the Lutheran World Federation and the (U.S.) Bishops' Committee for Ecumenical and Interreligious Affairs. He teaches theology at Catholic University, Washington, D.C.

Dr. Lindbeck is a Lutheran participant in the U.S. dialogues, as well as in the international dialogues sponsored by the Lutheran World Federation and the Vatican Secretariat for the Promotion of Christian Unity. He teaches theology at Yale University, New Haven, Conn.

1. The Creed

"In the name of the Father and of the Son and of the Holy Spirit." With those words, in holy baptism, we become members of Christ's body, the Church. From the beginning, our life as Christians is stamped by the name of the triune God. We belong to the people who hold that God is to be worshiped as Father, the creator and preserver of all things; as Son, Jesus Christ, who through his life, death and resurrection redeems us to be children of God; as Holy Spirit, the life-giver who calls people to faith, who comes to them through word and sacrament to forgive sin and grant eternal life. Belief in the Trinity is not just an intellectual commitment, but a confidence that God as Father, Son and Holy Spirit has shown us mercy and love. Into such a name have we been baptized.

Among Lutherans and Roman Catholics, trinitarian terms are used often: at the beginning and end of most services, in blessings, at the conclusions of prayers and elsewhere. Trinitarian faith is expressed when, Sunday after Sunday, the assembled faithful recite the words of the Nicene (or the Apostles') Creed. Although the two churches are divided by the events of the Reformation and more than four hundred years of separate history, our use of a common Creed is surely a powerful sign that we share one faith. It often requires no more than a visit by a Lutheran to a Roman Catholic service, or vice versa, to break down old prejudices and reveal how much we share.

How We Got the Creed

What, then, is this ancient document that unites us in spite of our divisions? Like the other creed of the Western Church, the so-

1

called Apostles' Creed, the Nicene Creed has its origins in the service of baptism. Neither Creed came about solely as an intellectual effort to explain the faith. Rather, both were bold confessions of faith made by believers at their baptism. The Apostles' Creed derives from a confession of faith in use very early — though after the time of the apostles—in Rome; hence its precise name is "The Old Roman Symbol."[1] The Nicene Creed seems to have had its roots in the third- and fourth-century baptismal creeds of the churches in Jerusalem and other Eastern cities. However, unlike the Apostles' Creed, its origins were not entirely liturgical. The Nicene Creed, as we now know it, was put in its final form at two great councils of the early Church.

The first council, from which this Creed receives its name, was held in 325 A.D. at Nicaea, a city near Constantinople (now Istanbul in Turkey). The council was called by the Emperor Constantine to settle a debate in the Church concerning the heresy of Arius, who taught that God the Son did not exist eternally with the Father. Arius taught that Christ was the first of God's creatures; in this belief he drew heavily on the philosophy of the neo-platonists who imagined a series of beings intermediate between the One (God) and our world. For orthodox Christians, neither the teaching of Arius nor its philosophical assumptions were tolerable because for them there could be but two kinds of being: God and his creatures. There was no room for being halfway between them. If Christ was a creature, he could not be God and, therefore, not truly our Savior.

Thus the Council of Nicaea insisted that Christ be called "true God from true God" and that the Son of God took flesh from the Virgin Mary and became also truly man. The great and saving mystery of the Christian faith is that God became a real human being, not that there exists a sort of half-human, half-divine superhero who helps us out of our difficulties. The Council of Nicaea spoke of the Son as "eternally begotten of the Father, God from God,[2] Light from Light, true God from true God, begotten not made, of one Being

---

[1] "Symbol" is a technical word for a credal statement. It comes from a Greek word meaning to gather together. A "symbol" gathers together and summarizes teachings. Curiously, its opposite is *diabolos,* the devil, whose Greek name means destroyer, disassembler, one who tears apart.

[2] "God from God" is a later Latin addition not in the original Creed.

with the Father. Through him all things were made." This language was designed to rule out any idea of the Son's being a creature. It affirms his eternal oneness with the Father, as when the Gospel of John (1:1) says: "In the beginning was the Word, and the Word was with God, and the Word was God." "Through him all things were made" echoes John 1:3 as well as other portions of Scripture, asserting that the Son himself could not have been a creature, since all things were made through him. The Nicene Creed proclaims the doctrine of the Trinity, of one God in three persons as we are accustomed (clumsily) to put it, but the Council of Nicaea itself settled a problem principally concerned with the person of Jesus Christ. It attempted to state more clearly the Christian belief that in Jesus of Nazareth the "fullness of God was pleased to dwell" (Col. 1:19).

The Council of Nicaea did not address itself to the teaching about God the Holy Spirit. The Creed approved at Nicaea ends with the words: "And in the Holy Spirit." The Creed which we recite is not precisely the same as the one approved at Nicaea. The concluding article on the Holy Spirit and the Church reached its final form at the Council of Constantinople, the second ecumenical council, in 381 A.D. With a few other revisions in wording, this is the Creed which we confess in our churches. The Council of Constantinople, in the last article of the Creed, stated that the Holy Spirit is one with the Father and the Son and that he is the truly divine life-giving Spirit. Because its final form was achieved at Constantinople, the precise name for our Creed is the Nicene-Constantinopolitan Symbol. Developed through a century's debate on the nature of the divinity of the Son and the Holy Spirit—and with roots in earlier baptismal liturgies—it is the one truly ecumenical Creed, held and confessed in the churches of East and West until this day.

The Creed's Authority Today

The approval of this Creed in its earlier form at Nicaea and in its present form at Constantinople, as well as its reaffirmation by the Council of Chalcedon in 451 A.D., establishes it as a dogma of the Catholic churches, both East and West. For the Roman Catholic Church, no further corroboration is necessary, since the Roman

Catholic Church accepts the magisterial (teaching) authority of the ecumenical councils down through the Second Vatican Council. Lutherans do not have such a precise understanding of the authority of councils—we will say more of this later—but the Lutheran Augsburg Confession is very clear in its first article: "We unanimously hold and teach, in accordance with the decree of the Council of Nicaea, that there is one divine essence, which is called and which is truly God, and that there are three persons in this one divine essence, equal in power and alike eternal: God the Father, God the Son, God the Holy Spirit." In this statement the Lutheran reformers, without speaking specifically of the authority of the council, affirmed the Nicene Creed and the catholic faith expressed in it. By that first article of the Augsburg Confession, it was assured that Lutherans would continue to confess the Creed and maintain a crucial bond of unity with the Roman Catholic community, even after the Reformation resulted in a division into two bodies.

What is established by this common confession of faith is more than an assent to similar principles—the way in which, for instance, assent to the United Nations Charter is intended to establish agreement in principle among the world's nations. The Nicene Creed establishes agreement in faith, which is something far deeper than principle. For Christians, faith means not only a belief that certain things are true about God and the world. It means that *I trust* in the God described in this Creed as the lover, creator, savior and deliverer of his people. What Lutherans and Roman Catholics share in the Nicene Creed is not only a common idea *about* God, but a common faith *in* God. It reflects a common faith about *who God is.* It reflects a common hope that God is the one who can restore a broken, sinful world and forgive and renew us. It reflects a common love for God who has done so much "for us and for our salvation." Although much of the language of the Creed is technical and difficult for some people to understand, its intention, particularly as we use it in worship, is praise of the triune God who has brought us life.

Dogma Is Inescapable

The Nicene Creed is a *dogma* of the Church, that is, a formally adopted and approved statement of true Christian teaching. It rules out contrary statements in the Catholic Church (of which Lutherans believe themselves a part).

The word "dogma" has not been popular in recent times. Dogma is seen by many people as the opposite of freedom, integrity and honesty. Many understand dogma as a form of repression of the individual mind, as something anti-human, anti-modern and anti-American. To them, few worse insults can be leveled than to call someone "dogmatic." For such people, dogma is old-fashioned and regressive and should be shunned. Some Protestant groups with a strong biblical orientation criticize creeds and dogmas for being extra-biblical. "No Creed but the Bible" has been their cry. For Catholic Christians, to whom the Creed is part of joyous worship in the presence of God, dogma is, of course, a more positive matter.

Modern Christians should also recognize that the critics of dogma are themselves dogmatic; they often have very strong assumptions and consider as mistaken those who do not share them. The most obvious case of dogma in the modern world is Marxist communism, which makes a number of sweeping faith-statements about what is good and bad and about what will deliver humanity from its woes. The mutual condemnations between China and Russia are a secular, modern-day version of the mutual excommunications of Christian groups in the past. While there are many factors involved in the Sino-Soviet split, Christians would miss a valuable lesson if they overlooked the way in which the international conflict is a debate about dogma, a severe disagreement about a once common but now divided faith.

Dogma appears elsewhere in modern life. In psychological theories, in sexual conduct, in views of race, in politics and in a host of other areas, people hold to rigid standards of belief which define for them and for their group who is "in" and who is "out," who is right and who is wrong, what is good and what is not. Indeed, we may argue that while many of the prevailing dogmas of the modern world are pernicious and harmful, Christian dogma brings faith and hope when it proclaims a loving and a forgiving God. In a world where self-serving dogmas are the order of the day, Christian dogma is other-serving. It is the story of God serving the best interests of the human race. In a culture where dogma is seen as restrictive, damaging and narrowing (often so viewed, ironically, by those who are themselves loyal to various dogmas), Christians see the dogma of the Creed as a liberating message of hope and life. None of the other dogmas of our day can make such an offer.

Creeds in the Bible

Very different is the argument against creeds presented by Christians who do not stand in the catholic liturgical and credal tradition as Lutherans and Roman Catholics do. These brothers and sisters in Christ are not enemies of belief, of course, but they question the need for credal statements. Frequently they charge that all such statements are superfluous, because the Bible itself is sufficient to instruct us in the truth of the faith. Their argument is sincere and devout, but it forgets that the Bible itself contains credal statements. Of these, the most basic is the one cited by St. Paul in 1 Corinthians: "Jesus is Lord." For the earliest Christians, that was a Creed, a statement made by the power of the Holy Spirit to demonstrate that a person was a believer. It is clear in the New Testament text that St. Paul is quoting a sentence used as a Creed.

Other evidences of creeds in the New Testament include the hymn quoted by St. Paul in Philippians 2. He speaks of Christ "who, though he was in the form of God, did not count equality with God a thing to be grasped, but emptied himself, taking the form of a servant; being born in the likeness of men and being found in human form, he humbled himself and became obedient unto death, even death on a cross. Therefore, God has highly exalted him and bestowed on him the name which is above every name, that at the name of Jesus every knee should bow, in heaven and on earth and under the earth, and *every tongue confess* that Jesus is Lord to the glory of God the Father." Note the clear credal character of the underlined words. Here also is the already-mentioned Creed: "Jesus is Lord." That brief statement was apparently so enshrined in the consciousness of the Church that it could be readily quoted in another piece of early Christian liturgy, the hymn in Philippians 2.

Another credal statement in the New Testament is quoted by St. Paul in 1 Corinthians 15. Paul makes it clear that this is a formula, an established way of confessing the faith in the resurrection, when he says: "I *delivered. . . .* what I *also received.*" Paul handed on, as it had been taught to him, the faith that "Christ died for our sins in accordance with the Scriptures, that he was buried, that he was raised on the third day in accordance with the Scriptures, and that he appeared to Cephas, then to the twelve. Then he appeared to more than five hundred brethren at one time, most of whom are still alive, though some have fallen asleep. Then he appeared to James, then to all the apostles." This is a Creed about the resurrection, a Creed older than the New Testament, which is cited by one of the New Testament writers as an authority.

Finally, there is the most ancient of all creeds, the Hebrew *shema:* "Hear, O Israel: The Lord our God is one Lord" (Dt. 6:4). That, too, is a confession of faith, one so revered in the Christian community that we could say, without stretching the point unduly, that our Nicene Creed is a commentary upon it. What the Nicene Creed does is to state how Christians continue to believe that God is really *one* when they acknowledge the *triune* nature of God as Father, Son and Holy Spirit. We might well maintain that the creeds are necessary to affirm clearly that Christians in their trinitarian faith have not veered from the old covenant profession of the oneness of God. Christians are trinitarians, not tritheists (believers in three gods).

Creeds among the "Creedless"

Lutherans and Roman Catholics find great value in the creeds, precisely because they faithfully summarize the biblical message. Even those who say they have no creed but the Bible tend to look for some standard of belief. One important example would be the conversion-experience which many Protestants call being "born again." Those who claim such a conversion affirm a unique experience of the presence and power of Jesus Christ in their lives. The confession that one has been "born again" asserts that Jesus is Lord for me. That is a credal claim.

Furthermore, many non-credal Christians, when they assert that the Bible is their sole standard of belief, make credal claims about the Bible. They confess that Scripture (usually meaning the sixty-six books common in the Protestant canon) is the inerrant word of God. Curiously, the words "inerrant," "infallible" and "plenary verbal inspiration," which are so commonly used, are not themselves biblical terms. They are traditional terms used to make dogmatic claims about Scripture.

Many "Bible Christians," especially the fundamentalists, hold to some set of basic dogmas which they use to distinguish themselves from others. The five fundamental teachings (virgin birth of Christ, his physical resurrection, his blood atonement, his return in glory, and the inerrancy of Scripture) that give the fundamentalists their name constitute a fairly precise Creed.

In brief, those who say they have no creeds tend to make credal statements, and those who say they oppose dogma are often likely to have dogmas of their own. Only those who truly do not care what anyone believes can be said to be free of dogma and creeds, but such persons are almost impossible to find among sane and sensible people. It is really not possible to be human without believing something, without believing that some things are more important than others, without valuing some things and not others, without caring deeply. Some theologians would argue that this means every human being believes in something, that is, puts trust and hope in something, whether God or false god.

Because we stand in the historic Christian Church—in communities both Lutheran and Roman Catholic—which seeks to be nourished by the witness of past and present, the Creed is an expression of what we believe and what we hope for: "We look for the resurrection of the dead and the life of the world to come." The Nicene Creed marks out for us the minimally-necessary assertions we must make if we are to look in hope toward the future prepared for us through the life, death and resurrection of Jesus Christ. These assertions are, first, that there is a God who made and truly preserves and loves our world, and, second, that Jesus Christ, who is truly and fully divine, became a real human being, lived, died, and rose again for us. Equally important is the assertion that through the life of the Church, God the Holy Spirit comes to us to make Christ's saving work available to us. Some imagine that the creeds are elaborate philosophical impositions of antique ideas upon a moderately superstitious and uninformed laity. For us, they are a brief statement of the purpose of our life. To confess the Nicene Creed is an act of worship of the triune God and a statement of the highest possible human hope.

The Creed's Relation to Scripture

When we say that, in addition to the Scriptures, creeds have value in the Church, we must be careful about what we mean. To make such a statement is not to say that the creeds are an addition to Scripture, but that they are an important, indispensable expression of Christian truth for the Church. Lutherans and Roman Catholics bow before the authority of sacred Scripture because in Scripture they find the record of God's saving work. Those who originally drafted and phrased the creeds had no sense of adding to Scripture or completing it, but only of summarizing and declaring what Scripture teaches.

The Nicene Creed, in particular, contains non-scriptural language adapted from the philosophies of the ancient world. A notable example is the Greek word *homoousios,* translated in our current English version as "of one Being." It wants to affirm that God the Son is truly one with God the Father, that he is fully divine, not a demigod or semi-god. The Arian heretics, against whom this Greek term was used, made a contrary assertion employing a term that differed only by one letter, *homoiousios,* which meant that the Son was of "like" substance with the Father, but not the *same.* The ancient bishops and theologians resorted to these philosophical terms to help clarify their thought. Although the words themselves are not scriptural, they were used to summarize the scriptural teaching about Christ's oneness with the Father. Martin Luther, on occasion, entertained doubts about the wisdom of using such non-scriptural language, but, on balance, he and those churches called Lutheran have assented gladly to the Catholic consensus that such terminology is both appropriate and necessary.

Still, it is important to understand that the creeds are not identical with the Bible. They put into organized, somewhat technical language, some truths that Scripture communicates through story, poetry, hymns and even ecstatic utterances. We believe that Jesus Christ is the true Son of God because the story of his birth, life, death and resurrection as told in the Gospels convinces us, and because what the Epistles say about him and his work moves us to faith. We believe that the Holy Spirit is the true Spirit of God because of scriptural testimony to the work of the Spirit in the early

Church. Because we have been called to faith through the Spirit's work, we have come to confess that the Spirit is life-giving.

In the Creed, we speak about relationships *within* the divinity, of the Son's being "eternally begotten," of the Holy Spirit's "proceeding." Scripture rarely lays it out in this way. Instead, it speaks about the work of the triune God or of the Father, Son or Holy Spirit, or it simply says the triune name as in St. Paul's blessings at the end of some of his letters, or in the baptismal formula found in Matthew 28:19. But the creeds are not merely an expression of a normal human tendency to try to organize everything and package it neatly. That propensity may indeed have had much to do with the development of creeds, but it surely does not need to be understood in a negative way. One very important aspect of faith is knowledge and understanding. Creeds are an aid to understanding; their efforts to organize the way in which we talk about God and confess our faith in him have been helpful to generations of believers.

The Creed and "Doctrinal Development"

As an attempt at summarizing and organizing biblical teaching, the Nicene Creed represents a process of doctrinal development. Not only did it put biblical teaching into orderly language, it also helped to clarify the Church's thought and led to further definition of Christian truth. The Nicene Creed itself is just such a definition. The framers of the Creed had no intention of doing something novel when they approved this document as a dogma of the Church. The Creed's statement does not *make* Jesus Christ the only-begotten Son of God; it only *states* that he *is.* However, the adoption of the Creed framed the mind of the Church so as to limit the way in which people might afterward speak about the sonship of Jesus Christ. Earlier, there were those who spoke as if Christ received his sonship at his baptism in the Jordan River or at his ascension to the right hand of the Father. Others, who were earlier perceived as perfectly orthodox, often had spoken of Christ as if he were in some way less than the Father. The development of Christian thought which led up to the Creed of Nicaea and Constantinople ruled out such other ways of talking about Jesus Christ. The councils passed a verdict against some of the theological ideas of the past and fixed the direction for the future.

In doing so, did they establish themselves as arbiters of the truth of Scripture? The answer would have to be "no," because they never felt themselves to be doing any such thing, and because the Church since then has agreed that they adequately expressed what Scripture revealed. In another sense, however, the answer would have to be "yes," if only for the simple reason that they stated what they thought the Christian truth was, over and against those who thought otherwise. As we survey the situation from the viewpoint of the twentieth century, they were certainly involved in a process of the development of Christian doctrine about the Trinity.

The idea that doctrine has developed has often frightened people. It seems to introduce a shakiness into Christian teaching. People often wonder what they dare to believe when they are confronted with the reality that things were not always quite the same as they are now. Most Christians tend to believe that the Church really is the way it was when they were children or when they became Christians. That is a common fallacy, but it is a fallacy nonetheless. Things were not always as they are now. To give a simple example, the Roman Catholic Church did not always worship in Latin. The earliest Roman Christians prayed and preached in Greek. For that matter, Lutherans did not always worship in the language of the people. Much of the Lutheran liturgy continued to be sung in Latin in many places until the eighteenth century. The notion that a true, once-for-all rendition of "my religion" was imbibed with mother's milk may be comforting, but it is not accurate. The Church on earth, like other historical institutions, is subject to shift, adjustment and about-faces. Thus, the Church and its doctrine have developed through the centuries. The Gospel itself, the message of God's totally undeserved love and mercy toward sinners, and the paschal mystery of Christ's death and resurrection are unchanging and eternally true, but the way in which the people of God proclaim and confess these truths does change.

The Church Lives in History—Not Outside

Roman Catholics with their teaching about divine tradition may be slightly better equipped to understand and comprehend this reality than Lutherans are. Lutherans, however, should realize that the Reformation that has made them a distinct movement and church was part of a process of doctrinal development. The Lutheran reformers spoke about faith and justification in ways that were different from even their closest theological predecessors. The Reformers proposed a more precise definition of the meaning of certain parts of Scripture than the Church had ever offered before. If the Lutheran reformers were correct, people had always become righteous before God through the faith given to them by the Holy Spirit through the preaching of the Gospel and the sacraments. What the Reformation intended was that this understanding had to be absolutely clear in the Church, and that it had to govern all of Christian life. Lutherans and Roman Catholics are still discussing that proposition today. That is the sort of process through which doctrine or dogma develops.

A proposition that is *not* being debated between Roman Catholics and Lutherans is that the Son is "of one Being with the Father." That expression, a product of doctrinal development, is accepted by both. That statement, conditioned and molded by the world of the fourth century, is for all of us a dogma, a formally adopted statement of divine truth. In agreeing to the doctrines of the Nicene Creed, both communities acknowledge the validity of the process of development that led up to the actions of the ecumenical councils themselves. Thus they show a readiness to believe that the Holy Spirit leads and speaks through the people of God in their effort to perceive the revelation of God more clearly. Churches that accept creeds recognize that God deals with his people through history. They need not try to escape to a spiritual state apart from history—in the Bible, a romantic view of the tradition or personal experience—to be able to affirm God's goodness, love and saving work, whether expressed in Bible, Creed or personal experience.

Creeds Are Not "Perfect"

None of this is to say that the historical process of doctrinal development is absolutely perfect. On the contrary, to understand that doctrines develop is to know that they are human and imperfect expressions. When we confess the Nicene Creed to be true, we do not confess it to be perfect. We do not say that it expresses every statement that it makes in the best possible way. Today we might choose different words and phrases at various points.

Some of the language of "being" and "begetting" could be expressed otherwise. Like Scripture, the Creed employs certain figures of speech that would be distortions if they were taken literally. For instance, the Nicene Creed speaks about Christ descending from heaven and ascending again. While Christ's departure from his disciples took the form of an ascension into the heavens, it is, of course, not the case that heaven, the seat of God's presence, is somewhere above the earth in the sense of physical distance or location. The earth is, after all, a sphere. God's heavenly kingdom is not restricted to a certain place. Likewise, when we speak of Christ sitting at the right hand of the Father, we do not imagine that God has a right hand as we do. We mean simply to say that Christ rules as one with his Father. The right hand of God is everywhere Christ rules. It would be a mistake to try to replace these strong verbal pictures with more abstract, less earthy language, but the presence of such figures of speech and of philosophical terms serves to remind us that our Creed is but a halting expression of the mystery of God's existence and love.

Our words convey the truth in such a way as to bring us to faith, but not in such a way as to exhaust the truth of God, a truth that remains inexpressibly beyond us. We know what we need to know, that the triune God has created us, saved us, and made us holy, but until the kingdom of God comes, we will not know all that we would like to know about what St. Paul calls the "deep things of God."

How Does a Creed Become "Dogma"?

So far, we have concentrated on the purpose, meaning and importance of the Nicene Creed in the Church. Because the Creed is common to Roman Catholics and Lutherans, and because it is central in the liturgical life of both, it was chosen to be the focus for the first of the Lutheran-Roman Catholic dialogues in the United States. The participants in the dialogue were able to assume, as they say in their first summary remarks: "We confess in common the Nicene faith." Because this was known to be true from the outset, the Nicene Creed provided a very fruitful place from which to begin dialogue.

However, the first dialogue was not about the substance and

meaning of the Nicene Creed as such. The topic was the specific question of the *status* of the Nicene Creed as a *dogma* of the Church. That is a somewhat technical theological problem quite different from the question of the truth of the Nicene faith. The discussion concerned the issue of what makes the Nicene Creed a dogma of the Church. It pondered why Lutherans and Roman Catholics dare to say that the Nicene Creed is a dogma of the Church, a teaching to which Catholic Christians are bound by conscience and confession. What makes it binding? As indicated earlier, there are differences between the Lutheran and the Roman Catholic positions on this question.

The Roman Catholic "Magisterium"

Roman Catholics possess a very clearly stated understanding of the magisterium, the "teaching office" of the Church exercised through bishops, councils and popes. In the magisterium, Roman Catholics see the on-going work of the Holy Spirit guiding the people of God through the reflection, teaching and decision of its pastoral leaders. Thus, in his essay prepared for the first dialogue, the late John Courtney Murray wrote that the authority of the creeds of Nicaea and Constantinople "as a rule of faith derives formally from the authority of the magistery of the Church, 'whose function it is to judge with regard to the true sense and interpretation of the sacred Scriptures' " (Council of Trent, ses. 4, DE 786). Later, Murray added by way of underscoring this point that "judgments of certainty belong to the magistery. And such judgments are certain because it is true to say of the Church . . . what is said of the Spirit himself: 'He will not speak on his own authority, but whatever he hears he will speak' " (Jn. 16:13).

This position says that the teaching office of the Church is capable, under the guidance of the Holy Spirit, of stating the truth about God. When the teaching office makes formal statements interpreting divine revelation, these, for Roman Catholics, are correct dogmas to be held by all, and the believer may be certain that in believing what the Church teaches he believes the truth. In answer to the formal question of how one can be assured that this dogma is true, the Roman Catholic Church answers that it is true because the Holy Spirit guides the Church and guarantees the truth of the Church's authoritative, dogmatic pronouncements. Many Lutherans have considered this position to be presumptuous, but it need not be understood in that way. What the Roman Catholic Church asserts is that the lively power of the Holy Spirit in the Church serves as a guarantee that the Church speaks truthfully when it authoritatively interprets Scripture.

Lutherans sometimes charge that the magisterium asserts itself as a judge over Scripture. As Roman Catholics see it, this is not the case. All they claim is that the Holy Spirit guides the people of God in understanding God's word. This is something which all Christians affirm in one way or another, although the way in which they believe it happens might be vastly different from the way Roman Catholics see it. In explaining this relationship between word and Spirit, John Courtney Murray writes: "The Word[3] still speaks to the Church through the written word of God which is also somehow outside of us, above the Church, like the Word himself, containing a revelation that is at once definitively given to the Church and never fully to be comprehended by the Church." Few Lutherans would find reason to dissent from that view of Christ's continuing authority over all that the Church says and does in his name.

Protestant Views of Spirit's Guidance

Where Lutherans dissent is in their understanding of how the Spirit actually enables the Church through history to hear, understand and teach the word of God correctly, to say nothing of promulgating dogmas. The simple fact is that Lutherans, for better or worse, do not have such a direct, straightforward explanation of the process by which the Holy Spirit guides the people of God into all truth.

Charismatic Christians, some of whom are found in both Roman Catholic and Lutheran churches, have an answer of their own, because they believe in the immediate, direct operation of the Holy Spirit in everyone who has received the baptism of the Holy Spirit.

[3] Here, Murray means "Word" as referring to Jesus Christ.

For them, this operation guarantees the truth of their understanding of Holy Scripture. For several reasons, however, their position is not acceptable to most Lutherans and Catholics. Some go so far as to deny the reality of baptism by the Holy Spirit; others would point out that, valid or not, the charismatic experience may guarantee an individual's understanding, but not a community's. What may be valid as one person's spiritual experience may not necessarily be an apt guide for an entire community. Moreover, claims of direct insight are characteristically marred by conflicting insights among those who claim to have them. Thus, while charismatic renewal may offer much in the way of renewed faithfulness and devotion, it offers little help in answering how we know what is truly the word of God. The spirits of those who claim a greater gift of the Holy Spirit than other Christians need to be tested in the same way as all other spirits and insights are.

While they lack a theory about how the teaching of Scripture becomes the teaching of the Church, most Protestant communions have obviously not opted for the views of the charismatics. Some have taken the position that the meaning of Scripture is whatever it means to the individual interpreter. This is very gratifying to independent-minded moderns, but it is not very sensible, since Scripture presumably does not have an infinity of messages but one message. Thus the notion that "every man is his own pope" must be rejected. Even if that notion were not extremely individualistic and ridiculously anarchical, it would still not serve the needs and life of the people of God, the community of faith.

Another option is that the meaning of Scripture is transparent to the believing community, so that in some way the formal doctrinal teaching of the Church may be regarded as certain. While no Protestants guarantee this process, as Roman Catholics do with their doctrine of the magisterium, this position is surprisingly similar to the Roman Catholic understanding that the Church, led by the Holy Spirit, has the assurance that it really speaks for God when it arrives at dogmatic conclusions. When, for instance, Lutherans claim that "Scripture interprets Scripture," they are in essence arguing that the meaning of Scripture is apparent to the properly informed interpreter. Interpretation is, therefore, a churchly process as much for Lutherans as it is for Roman Catholics.

Lutheran Assent to Councils and Confessions

The Lutheran understanding of the creeds of the Church catholic and of its own confessional writings involves an assumption that it is possible for the community of faith to express the teaching of Holy Scripture correctly. Plainly, Lutherans have no doctrine of the magisterium. Equally plainly, they believe that the Church *is* capable of teaching truth and of interpreting divine revelation truthfully. Thus, the first article of the Augsburg Confession is able to give its assent to the "decree of the Council of Nicaea." Although the Lutherans, then as now, possessed no developed doctrine of the authority of Church councils, in the first sentence of the Augsburg Confession, which, as it turned out, constituted Lutheranism as a distinct movement of the Church catholic, the Reformers assented to a decree of a council. Obviously, therefore, they affirmed Nicaea's authority in some measure. The third article of the Augsburg Confession deals with the doctrine of the Son of God, and in a similar way it gives acceptance to the decree of the Council of Chalcedon, although it does not mention that council by name. The one completely clear conclusion is that the Reformers did accept these decrees of the early councils.

In addition, there is the issue of how Lutherans understand their own confessional writings. Lutherans ascribe dogmatic authority to those sixteenth-century writings. Lutheran pastors and teachers are bound to their doctrines. Lutherans believe that these lengthy credal documents are true interpretations of Scripture. At their ordination, Lutheran pastors confess their belief that the "holy Scriptures are the written word of God and the only judge, rule and norm of faith and life." They also subscribe to the Lutheran Confessions "as true witnesses and faithful expositions of the holy Scriptures." Again, what is apparent is that Lutherans make the assumption that non-scriptural writings, that is, the creeds and confessions, must be recognized as correct statements of Christian teaching. What must also be assumed is that Lutherans believe the Holy Spirit was guiding the Church when those writings were being created. While there may be no specific doctrine like that of the magisterium which attempts to explain the process by which the Church comes to valid credal conclusions, it is beyond doubt that Lutherans believe that the

Church does in fact draw valid doctrinal conclusions. Accordingly, Lutherans accept the notion that dogma exists and, with it, the notion that heresy is a real possibility and not merely one of a variety of possible opinions.

Points of Dispute and Agreement

Do Lutherans in particular, and Protestants in general, suffer from some theological insufficiency because they cannot articulate how the Holy Spirit leads the Church into the statement of doctrinal truth? Or are Roman Catholics guilty of overstating the case when they try to determine and define the process of doctrinal definition more than is perhaps honestly possible? Such are the counter-charges of interconfessional conflict. They are also valid questions which cannot be dismissed or brushed aside cheaply. They are questions with which each family of faith must honestly struggle. Most Lutherans would tend to feel that the Roman Catholic case, while enticing, is overstated, and that the teaching office is not as obvious, or as infallibly correct, as Roman Catholics assume. In turn, Roman Catholics have some right to charge that Lutherans have failed to "come clean" about how it is that one gets from Scripture to binding interpretations of Scripture like the creeds and confessions that are so important to Lutherans.

It would be misleading to imply that there is somehow a "golden mean" between these positions, so that with enough good will a compromise could be hammered out. What is needed for further agreement is not so much a compromise as an effort to discover what assumptions are shared in each position.

It turns out that there are several areas of agreement. First, both assume the ultimate teaching authority of holy Scripture. Second, both assume that creeds are necessary, and that the Church is capable of making correct doctrinal statements. Third, both assume that the Holy Spirit guides the people of God in the pursuit of fuller understanding. Fourth, both believe that it is possible to subscribe to Church dogma with certainty and conviction. Fifth, neither believes that the process of credal development is contrary to Scripture. Sixth, neither believes that the process of credal development represents an addition to Scripture or is some new revelation, but both understand the process of doctrinal development as an unfolding awareness of what has already been revealed.

In conclusion, there is a strongly favorable point to be made about each position. Roman Catholicism faces squarely the fact that the Church creates dogma. With faith in the on-going work of the Holy Spirit in the Church, Roman Catholicism reaches the conclusion that the magisterial statements of the Church have the Spirit's guarantee. On the other hand, Lutheranism does not attempt to answer the difficult question of how the Holy Spirit guides the people of God, although Lutherans remain confident that the Spirit does guide them. In accepting the conclusions of the councils without having a doctrine about councils, Lutheranism finds itself in a curious agreement with the ancient Church. The Church of the early councils, that is, the Church of the first several centuries, did not have a doctrine of councils or of doctrinal development either. To this day, Eastern Orthodoxy also affirms the conclusions of the councils, although it lacks a doctrine of magisterial authority. Thus there endures in Lutheranism something of the early Church's confidence in the operation of the Holy Spirit within the Church, a confidence that felt no need for further definition.

A Positive Starting Point

While the first Lutheran-Roman Catholic dialogue in the United States did not achieve agreement about what makes the Nicene Creed a dogma of the Church, it did reveal agreement that the Nicene Creed *is* a dogma of the Church. The dialogue agreed that, at this very important level, Lutherans and Roman Catholics share a common faith. In that discovery, some grounds for a growing unity were established.

It is, of course, not as if this discovery were news. Both theologians and many informed clergy as well as lay people in both churches knew that this discussion would reveal significant agreement. Each community was aware of the other's position. It was not by accident that the dialogues began at this point, because the Nicene Creed provided a good, positive place at which to start. The dialogue began not with one of the old sources of conflict, such as the doctrine of justification, or the role of the papacy, but with something that would enable a constructive beginning. The theologians were not evading hard issues. On the contrary, they began with something that would reveal hard and genuine agreement between Roman Catholics and Lutherans, and, as we all know, it is sometimes more difficult to admit to agreement than it is to state disagreement. Roman Catholics admitted that Lutherans, even if schismatic, were not heretical in their teaching about the holy Trinity and Christ. Lutherans, in turn, suspended some of their classical polemics against Roman Catholicism's teaching about divine tradition and set out to discuss the Creed, a traditional document shared by both parties.

The commonality so readily revealed in these discussions obviously has great significance for Christians who find their spiritual home in one of these two communions. If we agree about who God is and what he has done "for us and for our salvation," then we are confronted with the reality that as Christians we have vastly more in common than we do in conflict. Furthermore, what we have in common is not merely a general sense of agreement, but this quite specific Christian statement of faith. In our very similar liturgies, we confess an identical Creed, and in that confession we acknowledge a unity that is greater than many Lutherans or Roman Catholics realize. For us now, the question is this: To which actual expressions of unity should our knowledge that we share a common statement of faith eventually lead us?

Where Do We Go from Here?

First of all, this knowledge should lead to a further decrease in suspicion and hostility between our churches. In recent years, most of us have experienced such a decrease, but too often it was not based on mutual understanding and appreciation, but instead on a contemporary sense that beliefs do not matter much. Lutherans and Roman Catholics hold that beliefs—Christian faith and credal statements, for instance—mean a great deal. If we are to be more gracious toward one another, that should be so, not because we do not care what anyone believes or teaches, but because we do care very much indeed. Since we do care about beliefs, we are greatly encouraged to discover that a statement of belief so fundamental as the Nicene Creed is already shared between us. Thus, our increasing mutual respect can be genuine, and not mere lackadaisical tolerance based on such vague notions as "There's only one God," or "It doesn't matter what you believe as long as you live right," or "All religions are good." There is indeed only one God, but God is not truly or rightly known and worshiped by every single person who accepts that idea. Lutherans and Roman Catholics agree about who that one God is: the God of Israel, the Father of our Lord Jesus Christ, the holy Trinity.

In addition to this decrease in suspicion and increase in mutual respect, the general agreement about the Nicene Creed which has been reached by the theologians has established a base for further dialogue among them. The remaining chapters of this book deal with the later dialogues and with what they achieved in further understanding and agreement. It is the hope that those who use this book will be moved to capitalize on the potential generated by the theological dialogues and enter into meaningful discussion with their neighbors, Lutheran or Roman Catholic, as the case may be. It is especially hoped that casual tolerance will be increasingly replaced by genuine affirmation of one community by the other. This can be achieved only by study, discussion and meaningful contact.

Finally, it must always be our hope that in contacts such as these we will find the increasing fulfillment of our Lord's prayer that "they may be one even as we (the Father and the Son) are one" (Jn. 17:22). The unity of the Church is not an option, but a command; it is not a matter of mere tolerance and agreement in principle, but of a single faith, life and witness. The division between Lutherans and Roman Catholics is a tragedy of Christian history, a tragedy desired by neither party. The Lutheran Reformation was not a declaration of independence, but a reform movement. Its suggestions were not acceptable to a large section of the sixteenth-century Church, and some of these suggestions are still being debated between us today. The separate existence of Lutheranism occurred because the majority of the Church at that time did not agree with the statement of the Augsburg Confession that nothing in it was "contrary or opposed to (the teaching) of the universal Christian Church, or even of the Roman Church (insofar as the latter's teaching is reflected in the writings of the Fathers)."

In the twentieth century, Lutherans and Roman Catholics may

be closer than they have ever been in the past to agreeing that they do, in fact, share a common catholic and evangelical faith. Just as the renewed emphasis on Scripture and preaching in the Roman Catholic Church since the Second Vatican Council has made that community more plainly evangelical, so a renewed understanding of its own roots has made Lutheranism increasingly aware of its catholicity. In studying the Nicene Creed, we find a common faith in the evangelical heart of the Creed's message about God's salvation through Jesus Christ and a common recognition of the catholic character of that ancient document developed by the bishops in Christian council.

Such recognition of oneness in the Gospel of Jesus Christ and in the catholic substance of doctrine and liturgy can only serve to bring us closer together. The days of mutual condemnation are clearly past, but what is more important is that we are in a time of mutual affirmation. We share a common faith confessed in the Creed, preached in our churches and lived in the hearts of the faithful. We share a common baptism in the name of the triune God whom we know as our Lord and Savior. And we hope for an increased sharing of all holy things between us—perhaps, before too long, even the very sacrament of Jesus Christ's body and blood.

FOR STUDY AND DISCUSSION

1. What are the several origins of the Nicene Creed?
2. What authority does the Creed have for Lutherans today? For Roman Catholics?
3. What is a "dogma"? Why is the Creed called a dogma?
4. What are some examples of creeds found in the Bible?
5. What is meant by the statement that "those who say they have no creeds tend to make credal statements, and those who say they oppose dogma are often likely to have dogmas of their own"?
6. What is the relationship that exists between creeds and the Bible?
7. What is meant by doctrinal development? What is the place of the creeds in the process of doctrinal development?
8. How are creeds affected by historical factors?
9. What is meant by the statement that "to understand that doc-

trines develop is to know that they are human and imperfect expressions"?

10. What was the central topic of discussion in the first Lutheran-Roman Catholic dialogue in the United States? What was its significance as a topic for discussion?

11. What is meant by the "magisterium"? What is its function and importance in the Roman Catholic Church?

12. How do Lutherans view the Roman Catholic "magisterium" and its role in the Catholic Church?

13. How do Protestants explain the process by which the Holy Spirit guides the Church and its members?

14. What is the status of confessional writings among Lutherans? How are those writings related to the Bible and to authority in the Church?

15. What are the several points of agreement among Lutherans and Roman Catholics concerning doctrine and its formulation? How do the two churches differ from one another in this regard?

16. What is the significance of the fact that the Lutheran-Roman Catholic dialogue in the United States agreed that Lutherans and Roman Catholics share a common faith regarding the Nicene Creed as a dogma of the Church?

17. What does the future hold for Lutheran-Roman Catholic relations as a result of their agreement about the Nicene Creed as a dogma of the Church?

FOR FURTHER READING

Don Brophy and Edythe Westenhaver, eds., *The Story of Catholics in America* (New York: Paulist Press).

Edgar M. Carlson, *The Classic Christian Faith* (Minneapolis: Augsburg Publishing House).

Paul C. Empie and T. Austin Murphy, eds., *Lutherans and Catholics in Dialogue I-IV* (Minneapolis: Augsburg Publishing House).

George W. Forell, *The Augsburg Confession* (Minneapolis: Augsburg Publishing House).

John L. McKenzie, *The Roman Catholic Church* (Garden City: Doubleday Image Books).

Philip E. Pederson, ed., *What Does This Mean? Luther's Catechisms Today* (Minneapolis: Augsburg Publishing House).

Sharing the Light of Faith: National Catechetical Directory for Catholics of the United States (Washington, D.C.: National Conference of Catholic Bishops).

Helmut Thielicke, *I Believe: The Christian's Creed* (Philadelphia: Fortress Press).

Willmar Thorkelson, *Lutherans in the U.S.A.* (Minneapolis: Augsburg Publishing House).

2. Baptism for the Forgiveness of Sins

"You were washed, you were sanctified, you were justified in the name of the Lord Jesus Christ and in the Spirit of our God" (1 Cor. 6:11). "As many of you as were baptized into Christ have put on Christ" (Gal. 3:27).

For both Roman Catholics and Lutherans, entrance to the Church is by way of baptism. A washing with water "in the name of the Father and of the Son and of the Holy Spirit" (Mt. 28:19) marks the beginning of our new life in Christ, the prerequisite of everything else we do in the Church. How can so much (our incorporation into God's gift of salvation) depend upon what appears like so little (a ritual act with ordinary water and a few simple words)?

Baptism Is a Sacrament

What Christ does, baptism does. That is why what we say about Christ, we also say about baptism. This is a common affirmation for both Roman Catholic and Lutheran Christians. We affirm that Christ is made known to us through human words and water of this earth. When the word of God is joined with water, that word-and-water is the sacrament of holy baptism.

By sacrament, Lutherans and Roman Catholics have meant a physical expression of God's word—a means of grace, an instrument of the Holy Spirit, an external word. A sacrament is nothing other than the word of God in sensual form: visible (tangible, edible, drinkable) as well as audible. Thus a sacrament, parallel to the coming of God's word in the human flesh of Jesus Christ, is both something of earth—water, bread, wine—and that which is of God—grace, the Holy Spirit, the word.

25

At this point Roman Catholics and Lutherans at least have agreed as to what ought to determine a sacrament of the New Testament. Together we have insisted that such a rite or ceremony have both command and promise from God, that is, be instituted by Christ for our salvation. Baptism unquestionably meets the criteria, and therefore is acknowledged to be a true sacrament of the New Testament.

Baptism in the New Testament

In the New Testament baptism is given a variety of descriptions: baptism of repentance for the forgiveness of sins (Mk. 1:4), baptism in the Holy Spirit (Mk. 1:8), baptism into the name of Christ (Acts 2:38, 10:43, 19:5; cf. Mt. 28:19), baptism into the death and burial and resurrection of Christ (Rom. 6:3–4; Col. 2:12), baptism into one body (1 Cor. 12:13; cf. Eph. 4:4–5), baptism of salvation (1 Pet. 3:21; Mk. 16:16).

Sometimes the language emphasizes the bathing as well as the plunging of baptism: washing in the name of the Lord and in the Spirit (1 Cor. 6:11), washing of water with the word (Eph. 5:26), washing of rebirth and renewal of the Holy Spirit (Tit. 3:5; cf. Jn. 3:3,5), bodily washing of clean water (Heb. 10:22).

Other descriptions include: clothing in Christ (Gal. 3:27), the circumcision of Christ (Col. 2:11–12), the seal of the spirit (2 Cor. 1:22; Eph. 1:13, 4:30), enlightenment (Eph. 5:14; Heb. 6:4, 10:32).

Even a cursory reading of these passages should help the Christian recognize that what we say about Christ, we also say about baptism. It is indeed not the water or washing, but rather the *for* or *into* or *of* character that qualifies baptism as a true sacrament of the New Testament: *for* the forgiveness of sins, *into* Christ, *of* the Holy Spirit. It is that which is *of God* that makes baptism a sacrament and allows us to say: What Christ does, baptism does.

Baptism Is an Incorporation and Initiation

From the New Testament descriptions we see that baptism is both an incorporation into Christ and an initiation into the kingdom of God. There is a quality to baptism—we might say a "real presence"—that includes both the past and the future. The Second Vatican Council put it this way: "By his power he is present in the sacraments, so that when a man baptizes, it is really Christ himself who baptizes" (*Constitution on the Sacred Liturgy,* 7; cf. Luther's *Large Catechism,* IV, 10).

So, when a person is baptized, the name of God, who is present then and there, is invoked: "In the name of the Father, and of the Son and of the Holy Spirit." That word-and-water baptism, by virtue of the invocation of the triune God, becomes a participation in the death, burial and resurrection of Christ and in the coming kingdom of God.

However, baptism is not simply a backward glance at the cross of Christ or a forward view toward the kingdom to come. Baptism qualifies as a sacrament precisely because the cross and the kingdom are truly present, here and now. Baptism has a dimension of participation in the future, outside of time, as well as in a past event of history. It is as though the past event of the cross were brought into the present, and the future coming of the kingdom infringed on the present.

It is this dimension to baptism into Christ that marked both its continuity with and its distinction from the baptism with which John baptized. John preached a baptism of repentance for the forgiveness of sins, to be sure, but he also pointed to the One coming who would baptize with the Holy Spirit. Perhaps more crucial was that John's baptism knew nothing of a baptism into the death, burial and resurrection of Christ.

Consequently, the New Testament descriptions of baptism strike a note that something crucial is happening. In view of the coming kingdom, the baptismal candidates are called first to repent of their sins, with the assurance of forgiveness and the promise of God's own Spirit. The sacred name of the Lord is invoked as they are bathed or plunged in the waters that cleanse or drown their sinfulness, again with the assurance of participation in the saving death, burial and resurrection of the Lord himself.

The baptized have passed through the waters: from sin to forgiveness, from death to life. Now they are signed and sealed with the mark of Christ (the sign of his cross) and the gift of the Holy Spirit (the laying on of hands and/or the anointing with oil). Again, they have passed from bondage as slaves of sin to freedom as children of God, from life under the control of demonic powers to life under the guidance of the Holy Spirit.

All of this is claimed for baptism because God who is present is stronger than all that which would separate and divide us. Thus we say that baptism is both an incorporation and initiation that overcomes our separation and divisions. To be baptized is to be called by Christ who has received authority to gather together all peoples who have been divided by forces and conditions both beyond and within themselves. To be baptized is to be joined with Christ who has achieved victory over all forces and conditions that would separate us from God who is love.

Such a dynamic understanding of baptism is necessary for healing the breach between Roman Catholic and Lutheran Christians. For the irony of the Augsburg Confession is that those who presented it and those who heard it acknowledged one baptism, yet have been separated and divided into Lutheran and Roman parties ever since the sixteenth century. Now, four hundred and fifty years later we still find ourselves separated and divided while we hold to a baptism that unites us to each other as well as to Christ.

The issue for contemporary Christians is unity in Christ—a unity that breaks down the barriers of race and religion, class and status, sex and title. That unity is of the essence of the Gospel. It is not an option. To underscore this the New Testament makes unity an article of faith: "One body and one Spirit, just as you were called in one hope of your calling; one Lord, one faith, one baptism; one God and Father of all, who is over all and through all and in all" (Eph. 4:4–6).

One Baptism for the Forgiveness of Sins

Given our contemporary situation, it is significant that baptism is first mentioned in the Augsburg Confession with reference to original sin. Immediately after affirming the Nicene confession of *one* God, it states: "All are born in sin." The unity of God is juxtaposed with the sinfulness of man.

What is this sin so original to all peoples? It is the age-old breaking of the first and foremost commandment: We do not fear, love or trust God above all things. Later on the Augsburg Confession speaks of this original sin as turning away from God.

Such separation leads to division. At least that is the observation which Genesis makes of Everyman. The road away from the garden of Eden inevitably winds its way to the tower of Babel. To turn away from God is to turn away from brother and sister. Adam's stealing from God's tree, Cain's killing of his brother, the violence throughout the world at the time of Noah, the dispersal of the Babel builders—all stem from their original disobedience, anger and lack of fear toward the Lord.

This sin condemns, the Church is bold to say, "all those who are not reborn through baptism and the Holy Spirit" (Augsburg Confession, Art. II). This too must be held in juxtaposition with the New Testament confession: "Baptism saves." Sin and baptism, condemnation and salvation are set in contrast one to the other, so that what is affirmed about one should be seen in the light of what is affirmed about the other. Neither is an absolute statement in and of itself.

Baptism is Necessary for Salvation

When the Church has reflected on baptism, it has concluded, in agreement with the New Testament: "Baptism saves." In the sixteenth century the Lutheran party affirmed this Catholic doctrine in the Augsburg Confession: "Concerning baptism, they teach that it is necessary for salvation" (Art. IX), and the Roman party likewise in the Council of Trent: "If anyone says that baptism is free, that is, not necessary for salvation, let him be anathema" (*Concerning Baptism,* Canon V).

At least two points are made when it is affirmed that baptism is necessary for salvation. On the one hand, the Church insists that baptism is not optional. It is not a matter of choice; we are not free to decline or ignore it. Rather it is an institution of God; it has God's own command. The opportunity we are given is to obey.

On the other hand, the Church claims that baptism is salutary. It does what it says it does. It is not a worthless washing in water. Rather it is a sacrament of God: it has God's own promise. What is given to us in baptism is everything that Christ has won for us on the cross.

"Through baptism is offered the grace of God." Thus baptism is described as a gracious and salutary water of life, a bath of new birth in the Holy Spirit, an incorporation into the crucified and glorified

Christ, a sharing of the divine life, a bond of unity linking all the baptized, a point of departure directed toward the fullness of life in Christ (cf. *Small Catechism,* IV, 10; *Decree on Ecumenism,* 22).

From its beginnings, the Catholic faith has been: "We acknowledge one baptism for the forgiveness of sins" (Nicene Creed). In baptism, it is claimed, divine forgiveness deals with human sinfulness. Again, what Christ has once accomplished on the cross is now made present in baptism.

Sin and forgiveness have become the generally descriptive words for that human condition and divine activity. That these are general terms is important for our understanding, lest we lose sight of other descriptions for the same human condition and divine activity, such as death and resurrection, bondage and liberation, alienation and reconciliation.

A comparison between the second article of the Creed and the benefits of baptism, using the *Small Catechism* of Martin Luther, may serve to illustrate both the variety of language in describing our redemption and the similarity in effect of the cross and our baptism. Through the cross "Jesus Christ has *released* me, a lost and condemned person, bought and won (*freed*) me from all *sins, death* and the power of the *devil* . . . that I might be his own, and live under him in his kingdom, and serve him in *eternal* righteousness, innocence and *salvation."* Baptism "works forgiveness of *sins, release*s (*free*s) from *death* and the *devil,* and gives *eternal salvation."*

Such a confession of faith, as proposed in these words from the *Small Catechism,* is certainly Catholic. We hear echoes of New Testament themes on incorporation into Christ and initiation into the kingdom, as well as the thrust of our passage from sin to forgiveness, from death to life, and from the devil to our Lord Christ. And no distinction is made between the effect of the cross and our baptism.

Children Are To Be Baptized

Once the Church has claimed "that through baptism the grace of God is offered," it becomes logical to affirm "that children are to be baptized." And by children is meant infants in particular. That is to say, the newborn are to be born anew.

In the life of Jesus we see a particular regard for children (Mk. 5:21–24, 35–43; 7:24–30; 9:14–27). They too participate in the liberation from evil and the resurrection to life which Jesus offers to everyone else. Sometimes they are represented by a single child whom Jesus sets in the midst of disciples (Mk. 9:36). Sometimes they are a sign of discipleship for elders who in turn are called "little ones" (Mt. 18:6, 10, 14). At other times they are explicitly mentioned as infants, probably carried in the arms of parents (Lk. 18:15).

Throughout Jesus' life there is a welcome for children, and an example is made of their obviously lowly condition—not as a prerequisite for entrance into the kingdom of God, but as an indication of God's overwhelming gracious activity—not unlike the reception Jesus gives tax collectors and prostitutes. Even the least is not outside the realm of the cross.

Whether or not the apostolic Church actually baptized children cannot be demonstrated absolutely from the New Testament. Undoubtedly there are some accounts which lead one to think that the households' baptized included children as well as parents (cf. Acts 2:39; 10:2, 48; 11:14; 16:15, 31, 33; 18:8). Regardless, the liturgical tradition of Western Catholic Christians has been to make use of the story of Jesus blessing the children as an appropriate reading at the baptism of infants (Mark 10:13–16).

The juxtaposition between sin which condemns and baptism which saves is also an important reason for baptizing children. For the claim is that all are sinful and consequently that all are in need of salvation. Our sinfulness has a universal, not simply an individual, dimension. This corresponds with the equally universal dimension to the saving activity of God in Christ. As our children are not outside the realm of his cross, so they are not beyond our common sinfulness. "Through baptism they are offered to God and received into God's grace" (Augsburg Confession, Art. IX).

Baptism and Repentance

What happens to those who sin after their baptism? A consistent answer throughout the history of the Church has been that through repentance they may receive forgiveness of sin. Such an answer makes it clear that, while the Church recognizes the once-for-all character of baptism, it also recognizes the universal character of sin.

Sin, death, the devil—all those forces of opposition continue to fight from within and outside us. There is no place to hide or escape from our common sinfulness. Sin is both perverse and pervasive.

Regardless, baptism endures. The promises held out to us when we were initially bathed or plunged still hold true. Because baptism is a sacrament of God, God who is present continues to honor the promises made. Though we may fall or fail, God is faithful and trustworthy.

The promised effect of baptism is forgiveness of sin. God keeps that promise of forgiveness, in spite of our prodigal nature to turn away from him. Because God is known for being steadfast in love, he also acts on our behalf to make his forgiving love known again and again. Sometimes he is compared to a shepherd seeking a lost sheep, or to a woman searching for a lost valuable, or to a father who runs after his wayward son (Lk. 15).

Again, on this point Roman Catholics as well as Lutherans can agree with the affirmation of the Augsburg Confession that all who have sinned after baptism, "at any time they come to repentance, may receive the forgiveness of sins, and to them absolution should not be denied by the Church" (Art. XII).

On this very point the Church wants it understood that repentance is a means of grace. Consequently, repentance is no more our work than baptism is. To view repentance simply as a change of heart or a mental exercise on our part is to take it out of the realm of God's grace.

Rather, both Lutheran and Roman Catholic Christians insist on a sacramental quality to repentance. Roman Catholics have held absolution or the sacrament of penance to be one of seven divinely instituted sacraments of the New Testament. Lutherans have not been so precise in the way they number the sacraments, but the Lutheran confessions do call absolution a "sacrament" and see it as an individual proclamation of God's word (parallel to public preaching in Scripture and sermon). For both groups, absolution is grounded in baptism (a return to baptismal grace) and is often used preparatory to Holy Communion.

Repentance Is a Return to Baptism

As baptism does what it says, so absolution does what it says—namely, forgive sins. As always with the means of grace, it is both a word from God and a word addressed to people. And as always with the word of God, it promises what it commands. The preaching of repentance in the name of Christ, the baptism of repentance for the forgiveness of sins, the blood of the covenant for the forgiveness of sins—all are effective instruments through which the Holy Spirit works faith in God who is faithful, trust in God who is trustworthy.

Likewise, repentance is claimed by Roman Catholics and Lutherans to be an effective instrument through which the Holy Spirit both awakens and strengthens faith among the baptized. And as a means of grace, repentance assures us that God is gracious and favorable toward us, forgiving sin, consoling conscience, freeing from fear.

Today, the sacrament of repentance is often referred to as reconciliation. That term says much about our relationship as sisters and brothers who have been baptized into Christ. Without denying the once-for-all character to baptism, reconciliation reminds us of the forgiving that must be going on long after our baptism.

To be sure, Christ has liberated us from the barriers that separate and divide us. But in another sense that liberation becomes effective in our daily lives when races, classes, sexes, religious groups, status-seekers, and title-holders are reconciled one to another.

To heal the breach of the sixteenth century is to reconcile Lutheran and Roman Catholic Christians. In other words, both parties need to come to repentance so that they may receive absolution or forgiveness of sin as from God himself.

Such is the approach we dare to take in the Lord's Prayer. If we are so bold as to pray for forgiveness for ourselves and each other before our Father, perhaps we could be a little more bold in our mutual conversation and consolation with each other. And when this kind of reconciliation takes place, the Church should in no way withhold the word of God which would be favorable toward such sinners who repent of their brokenness with one another.

Here, the significance of baptism for our daily lives comes to light. For repentance is a return to our baptism—a daily drowning and burial of all our sins, and a rising and living before God in righteousness and innocence forever. Through repentance we come full circle to the liberating event of the cross and our baptism. The lost are found, sinners are forgiven, righteousness is granted, and innocence is restored. No wonder there is joy in heaven and feasting on earth.

Baptism in the Worship of the Church

Baptism is a sacrament to be celebrated, not simply a doctrine to be professed. In the New Testament and in the Church we have heard baptism described and taught primarily in verbs of action. *Washing* of water with the word, *sealed* with the Holy Spirit, children *offered* to God and *received* into his grace—this is the language of celebration.

Here, too, Roman Catholics and Lutherans share a rich and common heritage. Even at the time of the breach in the sixteenth century, baptism in churches of the Lutheran party would have been scarcely distinguishable from baptism in churches of the Roman party except for language—the former using the vernacular, the latter retaining the Latin.

The celebration began with exorcisms of the demonic, the sign of the cross and prayers for the candidate's spiritual rebirth. The Gospel of Jesus blessing the children was often read, followed by the Lord's Prayer. Then a procession to the font marked the transition from the preceding remnants of making a catechumen to the final act of baptismal initiation.

The devil was renounced and faith in Father, Son and Holy Spirit confessed. Upon answering the question of desire for baptism, the candidate was bathed or plunged in water "in the name of the Father, and of the Son, and of the Holy Spirit." Having been clothed in a christening robe, the confirmation prayer for the Holy Spirit was said over the candidate. Finally all departed with the sign of peace.

We are inheritors of this common celebration of baptism. We have also come a long way. No longer are baptisms private ceremonies for family and friends on an afternoon in a corner of the church. Rather baptism among both parties today is a public celebration within the worshiping congregation, preferably at the parish Eucharist.

Baptism and Easter

If the Eucharist is the preferred setting for baptism, then Easter is a particularly appropriate occasion for its celebration. In the Bible readings, prayers and hymns appointed for Easter, our baptismal incorporation into Christ is brought into sharp focus.

The Bible readings proclaim the resurrection of Christ and remind us of our own passage from death to life through the waters of baptism. The prayers speak of those who have been reborn as children of God, enlightened with truth, and joined to the Church—all phrases which recall the meaning of our own baptism.

Two of our favorite Easter hymns—the one from the Eastern Church, "Come, you faithful, raise the strain of triumphant gladness," and the other from the Western Church, "At the Lamb's high feast we sing"—describe our baptism as an exodus through the sea and as a triumph over death.

Sometimes we call this Easter event the *paschal mystery.* We do not mean a well-kept secret, but rather a way in which God has made known what his will is for us and how we might share in doing it. That will is life; the way is through the cross. "Israel's hosts triumphant go through the wave that drowns the foe." "God has brought his Israel into joy from sadness."

"Thus, by baptism, men are plunged into the paschal mystery of Christ; they die with him, are buried with him, and rise with him" (*Constitution on the Liturgy* 6).

Whatever stands in opposition to God's will for his people must be destroyed, whether that be Pharaoh or Satan, slavery or sin. Then, on the other side—of the sea, of the cross—God holds out the life he desires for us: freedom from slavery, forgiveness of sin, resurrection of the dead.

We call this Easter *paschal:* having a sense of both the exodus and the Easter event—the passage of Israel from bondage to liberation and of Christ from death to life. We call this event a *mystery:* having a sense of participation in a past event of history—not only our ancestors, but also we ourselves have come out of Egypt—and a participation in the future coming of our own resurrection from death to life.

Therefore, we say that the paschal mystery is Christ himself (1 Cor. 5:7). He is the paschal lamb whose blood sets us free and makes us one. He is both the lamb of God and the shepherd of the sheep, who breaks loose from the shackles of hell and leads us out with shouts of joy. In him all creation is joined in unity: night and day are as one, heaven and earth are united, hatred and prejudice are destroyed, peace and harmony are restored. For Christ has broken down the barriers that separate and divide us.

Baptism as Christian Initiation

Baptism is the sacrament of initiation, the first door to grace. In biblical terms baptism would be described as an incorporation into Christ and an initiation into the kingdom of God. Since the Church is the body of Christ and the sign of the kingdom, baptism is consequently "the sacrament of initiation into the community of faith."

With this understanding of baptism as initiation, Roman Catholics and Lutherans are putting a greater emphasis on preparation for baptism than they have in the past four hundred and fifty years. This renewed emphasis on the initiation process squares well with the words of our Lord: "Make disciples of all peoples, baptizing them in the name of the Father and of the Son and of the Holy Spirit, teaching them to obey everything that I have commanded you" (Mt. 28:19–20).

In its early years the Church tried to maintain the triple action implied in making disciples, baptizing them and teaching them. Already in the New Testament we have an indication of the direction the Church would take: preliminary instruction of learners called catechumens instead of disciples (Gal. 6:6), and baptism, followed by the teaching of the apostles, the common life, the breaking of bread and prayer (Acts 2:41–42).

As the Church's mission became more complex, so its initiation process became more elaborate. Catechumens came from different areas of society, more often influenced by pagan than Jewish ways of living. Thus the stress on a life-style obedient to God's will increased in importance. The process more than informed; it actually introduced people into a new way of life.

When children, and particularly infants brought by parents, became the usual candidates for baptism, the preliminary catechumenate faded into oblivion. As a consequence, most catechetical instruction started to occur after the baptism of the candidates, and in the case of children, when they had reached an age of discernment. Faced with such a situation in the sixteenth century, Martin Luther wrote his still popular catechism for the instruction of children who had already been baptized as infants.

In our own day the Second Vatican Council has ordered a restoration of the catechumenate and a revision of the baptismal liturgy. The new Rite for Christian Initiation outlines a total process for baptismal candidates in Roman Catholic parishes. After several years as a catechumen, the candidate is enrolled for a final period of intensive instruction during Lent. Then at Easter the candidate is baptized and confirmed and receives Holy Communion. This rite is intended for adults and youth of catechetical age. A separate rite is provided for the baptism of children.

Lutherans have taken some similar steps. Catechism and catechumen are terms used in reference to the confirmation of youths already baptized as infants, who have been instructed in the faith and desire to affirm their baptism. This affirmation of baptism, or confirmation, is distinct from the sacrament of baptism. It is viewed neither as a sacrament itself, nor as a completion of baptism. In the *Lutheran Book of Worship* there is only one liturgy for baptism, whether the candidates are children or adults.

Confirmation for Roman Catholics is a sacrament which, like baptism, cannot be repeated. Its essence is the anointing with oil called chrism and the words: "Be sealed with the gift of the Holy Spirit." It marks the completion of Christian initiation for those who were baptized as infants or young children.

Yet for both of us confirmation has a strong connection with baptism. "For this reason it will be fitting for candidates to renew their baptismal promises just before they are confirmed" (*Constitution on the Sacred Liturgy* 71)—"thus underscoring God's action in their baptism" (*Lutheran Book of Worship,* Affirmation of Baptism 3).

The Liturgy for Baptism

As more baptisms are celebrated at the parish Eucharist, more of us will witness the rich and common heritage we share. There is a new sense of joyful celebration which echoes the triumphant character of Christ's resurrection. There is a renewed emphasis on the shared life in the community of the faithful which bears witness to the gifts of God's Spirit. There is a greater appreciation for the things of creation—water, light, oil, and the touch of human hands, as well as the human voice.

Naturally, our liturgies for baptism follow the common order we have inherited from days before the breach of the sixteenth century. However, our own ecumenical age has also influenced the way in which we baptize. We have learned from one another as well as received from our common spiritual ancestors.

The place of the word of God is central in our celebrations. Not only adult candidates, but also parents of child candidates are to be instructed beforehand. That catechetical instruction will certainly be grounded in the history of salvation. For those are the themes of the faith we profess: God and creation, Christ and redemption, the Holy Spirit and the Church. Even if baptism should be celebrated outside of the parish Eucharist, it is to happen only after the reading of Scripture.

The baptism of children is still the most common form among Roman Catholic and Lutheran Christians. Both of us have revised our liturgies for baptism, and the similarities are great.

In the context of Bible readings and intercessory prayer—the liturgy of the word in the parish Eucharist—the children are presented by their parents and sponsors, and the latter are charged with "the responsibility of training them in the practice of the faith."

At the font a prayer of thanksgiving is offered over the baptismal waters. This prayer recounts the history of salvation in fashion similar to the eucharistic prayers but with an emphasis on God's saving activity through the waters of the flood, the Red Sea and the Jordan River. The words of institution of baptism are set in the middle of the prayer, followed by the invocation of the Holy Spirit.

Then, just before the baptism, the baptismal group is asked to "reject sin and confess the faith of the Church, the faith in which we baptize." Now comes the climax: the children are baptized with water "in the name of the Father, and of the Son, and of the Holy Spirit"—just as candidates have been baptized from the beginnings throughout the world. For both Lutherans and Roman Catholics, baptism may be by pouring or by immersion into water.

After the baptism follows the prayer for the Holy Spirit, accompanied by the sign of the cross and anointing with oil (chrism). The baptized "have been sealed by the Holy Spirit and marked with the cross of Christ forever." Finally, they are clothed in white garments and given a lighted candle. Then follows the liturgy of the Eucharist.

Unity and Differences

Although "we acknowledge one baptism for the forgiveness of sins," there are differences for Lutherans and Roman Catholics to overcome. To be a sponsor or godparent differs between the churches and between parishes. While Roman Catholics might be accepted as sponsors by some Lutheran parishes, at present Lutherans may serve only as witnesses and not as sponsors in a Roman Catholic parish.

Both of us refuse to rebaptize since we accept baptism with water in the name of the triune God regardless of Church or administrator. Consequently, we both approve the practice of emergency baptism by any Christian. The Roman Catholic practice of "conditional" baptism is an attempt to affirm the oneness of baptism, but it is sometimes misunderstood as a second baptism.

What happens to the unbaptized is a difficult question for both of us with our double insistence on the necessity and the universality of the cross for salvation. The Roman Catholic theological opinion about limbo for the unbaptized infant is an attempt to affirm the graciousness of God, but is confusing and questionable to other Christians.

Nonetheless, we should be able to concur with our theologians "that the teachings of our respective traditions regarding baptism are in substantial agreement" (*Lutherans and Catholics in Dialogue* II). Thus we can agree on the gift of unity already given in baptism. To make that gift of unity visible in our life together is our continuing task and prayer.

FOR STUDY AND DISCUSSION

1. Read in the Bible the references cited in this chapter, noting carefully the context. Also read the articles cited from the Augs-

burg Confession and *Small Catechism,* and from the documents of Vatican II.

2. Using the holy baptism rite from the *Lutheran Book of Worship,* and the Roman Catholic Rite for Christian Initiation, make a parallel chart or listing of the elements in the two churches' baptismal liturgies, underscoring key words that are similar. What differences, if any, do you detect in the two forms of baptism?

3. How do Lutherans and Roman Catholics define the term "sacrament"?

4. How does Christian baptism relate to the baptism practiced by John the Baptist?

5. What are some of the "before" and "after" terms used in Scripture to describe the change that takes place when a person is baptized?

6. What are the reasons for the claim that "baptism is necessary for salvation"?

7. Both Lutherans and Roman Catholics customarily baptize infants. Some other Christians have rejected this practice, and even a few voices within our two churches are questioning whether, in the modern world, it is appropriate. Discuss this issue in the light of this chapter. What does our two churches' practice say about the nature of the Church as we understand it?

8. Discuss the customs surrounding baptism in your parishes and/or ethnic groups. Do you feel these customs enhance or detract from the meaning of baptism?

9. What are the duties of baptismal sponsors and/or witnesses in the two churches? Who may serve in this responsibility, and what qualifications must they possess?

10. What are "emergency baptism" and "conditional baptism"? Under what circumstances would either be used among Roman Catholics and among Lutherans?

11. How do Roman Catholics and Lutherans deal with sin committed after one has been baptized?

12. What are the various forms in which the "sacrament of penance" and "confession and forgiveness" are used among Roman Catholics and among Lutherans? Compare the forms used for them in the liturgical books of the two communions.

13. Why is baptism especially linked to Easter and the paschal mystery?

FOR FURTHER READING

A New Catechism: Catholic Faith for Adults (New York: Seabury Press).

Eugene Brand, *Baptism: A Pastoral Perspective* (Minneapolis: Augsburg Publishing House).

Oscar Cullmann, *Baptism in the New Testament* (Philadelphia: Westminister Press).

Paul C. Empie and T. Austin Murphs, eds., *Lutherans and Catholics in Dialogue I-IV* (Minneapolis: Augsburg Publishing House).

Martin E. Marty, *Baptism* (Philadelphia: Fortress Press).

The Common Catechism: A Book of Christian Faith (New York: Seabury Press).

3. Holy Communion

"The cup of blessing which we bless, is it not a participation in the blood of Christ? The bread which we break, is it not a participation in the body of Christ? . . . For as often as you eat this bread and drink the cup, you proclaim the Lord's death until he comes" (1 Cor. 10:16; 11:26). Both Roman Catholics and Lutherans participate in a sacred meal as a central feature of their worship of God. Both communities of believers confess that this sacrament relates the Church with the life, death, resurrection and second coming of Jesus Christ. They have used various terms for this meal and the liturgical form in which the meal is embedded—Lord's Supper, Holy Communion, Mass, Eucharist, Sacrament of the Altar. Both take seriously the mandate of Jesus which he gave "on the night in which he was betrayed" to "do this" in his memory.

In spite of their common eucharistic heritage and practice, the two churches have taken quite different paths since the time of the Reformation. In answer to important questions about the nature and use of this sacrament, they have given quite different replies. Their church disciplines have also prevented them from sharing the eucharistic meal with one another. Despite great ecumenical advances in the past few years, glaring disunity persists at the table of the Lord. It is a paradox, if not a contradiction, that this sacrament, which signifies and ensures the Church's growth in faith, is a point of scandalous division among Christians.

Common Liturgical Tradition

Until rather recently, the differences between a Roman Catholic Mass and the Lutheran Order for Holy Communion were so apparent that an observer would not recognize that they had the same source. In fact, they were and are quite similar. Both depended on the text of the Roman Mass as it was celebrated on the eve of the Reformation. At that time, the rite was conducted in Latin, which was poorly understood by ordinary folk, at an altar placed some distance from the congregation. The people generally were passive, and even if they followed the service at all, they participated only by observing the priest's actions. Few tried to understand the words of the service. Even fewer received Communion. Minimal attention was given to the scriptural passages read at the Eucharist, and when the clergy did manage to preach, they often did not use the day's Scripture as the source for their sermon. The Sunday Eucharist was central to the piety of Christians in the early sixteenth century, but that piety was quite passive and individualistic in its nature.

Martin Luther took the existing Roman Catholic liturgy and adjusted it in such a way that more emphasis was placed on participation and understanding. Hymns in the vernacular were introduced, the sermon was given a primary role in the Sunday service, and people were encouraged to receive Communion under the forms of bread and wine. The canon of the Mass (the prayer of consecration pronounced over the bread and wine) was drastically altered so that only the part referring to the institution of the Eucharist remained. Luther was vehemently opposed to any sacrificial references in the canon because he felt that such terminology promoted an understanding of the Eucharist as a purely human "good work." He emphasized the Eucharist as a gift received from God rather than as a sacrificial offering made to God by the community. The Council of Trent, however, standardized the text and ceremonies of the Mass for Roman Catholics to a greater extent than ever before. From this juncture, the Lutheran and Roman Catholic orders of service began to assume their distinctive shapes.

The New Mood

As a result of the liturgical reforms initiated by the Second Vatican Council, the Roman Catholic Church has dramatically changed the way in which the Mass is celebrated. At first these reforms seemed to make the Catholic liturgy appear very "Protestant" because many of the new features were also found in the Lutheran and Reformed orders of worship. However, those changes were based on a tradition which is far earlier than that of the sixteenth century. Some of the more significant changes that have recently been made in Roman Catholic worship include the use of the language of the people, greater attention to the Word, more emphasis on the reception of the Eucharist (with increased allowance for the use of both bread and wine), and a reduction in the number of Masses which priests celebrate "privately."

Such reforms in Roman Catholic practice have aided the progress of ecumenical dialogues concerning the Eucharist, because what were once seemingly unbridgeable differences in the liturgical life of the churches have now been overcome. One need only recall the firm language used in the Augsburg Confession about the importance of receiving the Eucharist under both kinds and about the "abomination" which the multiplication of "private" Masses was said to be (Art. 24) in order to realize that liturgical progress in the Roman Catholic Church has now transformed once fiercely debated issues into merely peripheral matters of concern. Such commonality will certainly promote ecumenism because theoretical agreements and common understandings of theological issues are actually being demonstrated in the liturgies celebrated by local congregations. The pastoral point is not that Roman Catholics are becoming more "Protestant" in their liturgy. Rather, these similarities show that there has been growth in understanding the importance of a liturgy in which people can truly participate, one which they can vividly experience as being the worship of the entire Church.

Just as Roman Catholic worship has not remained static since the sixteenth century, neither has Lutheran worship. From the viewpoint of the Church's understanding of the Eucharist, it is particularly significant that the eucharistic prayer (or great thanksgiving) has developed similarly in both the Lutheran and the Roman Catholic churches. Luther abbreviated the original Roman canon and removed all its sacrificial terminology; only the brief text of the institution narrative remained. Now this short text has been expanded, and alternative prayers of praise and thanksgiving have been provided. As a result of scholarly work in this area, the new thanksgiving prayers are more adequate expressions of praise, blessing and thanksgiving. They are often interspersed with acclamations by the congregation. They contain new passages invoking the Holy Spirit and expanded sections which more clearly relate the Eucharist and the mystery of Christ's life, passion, death and resurrection. It is interesting that some Lutherans have reacted to the changes by saying that such alterations have made their liturgy more "Catholic."

At the same time there have been similar changes in the Roman Catholic liturgy. Three new eucharistic prayers have been added to supplement the previously unchanging Roman canon. Like the new Lutheran prayers, these texts contain acclamations for use by the people and invocations of the Holy Spirit. They are generally regarded as better developed prayers of praise and blessing than the original canon was. Also helpful is the introduction of three new eucharistic prayers which can be used at Masses for children. The clear proclamation of the eucharistic prayer by the celebrant is important because the worshiping community can now participate in the prayer by attentive listening and by singing the acclamations. Not long ago Roman Catholics remained silent throughout the canon and could not even hear the words of the prayer because it was said silently by the celebrant in Latin.

From an ecumenical viewpoint, it is significant that both churches currently have one prayer that is very similar in its content. Both have taken a text from the third century and made it the basis for their contemporary revisions. Again, similarities far outweigh the differences which were formerly so apparent.

Drawing on a Wider Tradition

Both churches have made adjustments in worship that are rich theologically and liturgically; these are not just "changes for the sake of change." In order to proceed in a positive direction, both churches had to move beyond positions adopted in the sixteenth century. In that era of controversy, Lutherans were very concerned to abbreviate the Roman canon, and Roman Catholics wanted to keep that prayer intact as a privileged expression of their faith. In the recent reform, each church has used other, more ancient sources of liturgical tradition in order to discover what was lacking in its own eucharistic prayers. Both Lutherans and Roman Catholics have made significant changes in their eucharistic prayers and they are now very similar. However, it is important to note that the similarity is not the result of mere borrowing from one another. Rather, both churches realized that their liturgical expressions at the time of the Reformation were inadequate. That is to say, both churches examined their own tradition as well as the entire history and tradition of the Christian Church in evaluating their liturgical prayers. That wider tradition was seen to be far more extensive than anything either party had experienced in the sixteenth century. Both looked to the prayers of the early Church and used that tradition in making the current reforms. Such reforms are not merely for the satisfaction of historians. Rather, the eucharistic prayer is the prayer that contains what the Church believes about the Eucharist. To read and meditate on these prayers can help local congregations appreciate this important witness of faith.

Two significant conclusions can be drawn from the recent liturgical changes. First, the reforms show the dependence of each tradition on the other in improving its liturgy. An obvious example is the recent Roman Catholic emphasis on the Word, on the one hand, and the adoption by Lutherans of a new lectionary based on the Roman Catholic version, on the other. Such changes reveal great similarity and commonality precisely because each church was willing to borrow from the other. Secondly, both the Lutheran and Roman Catholic churches have come to understand theoretically and to experience pastorally the fact that liturgy is not fixed and does not always have to remain the same. Both churches have come to appreciate the necessity of continuing liturgical reforms.

The implications for ecumenism are enormous because the churches now admit their former weaknesses as well as the need to look beyond their own traditions in developing more adequate liturgical forms. Both can admit inadequacies and problems in eucharistic practice and seek assistance from one another. Both are able to draw upon the earlier traditions of worship which preceded the Reformation. Once these possibilities are understood, ecumenical progress is possible on the basis of more than mere comparison of past or present liturgies. Progress can be achieved by undertaking a common search beyond common problems toward a resolution that is necessary for the continuing vitality of worship in both churches.

One practical effect of this approach to dialogue is that church members will become less and less concerned about how "Protestant" or "Catholic" their liturgies have become as the result of recent reforms. Instead, they can concentrate on how their new liturgies show a greater unity than ever before. The present ways in which both churches worship give impressive witness to the agreement that is now possible between churches whose differences in worship were once unfortunate expressions of division.

Implications for Theology

When Roman Catholics and Lutherans discussed the Eucharist in dialogue during the past fifteen years, it became apparent that their different understandings of the sacrament were strongly influenced by their personal experiences of worship. The national dialogue which issued a statement on the Eucharist in 1967 and the international commission whose statement was published in 1978 have considered both liturgical matters and eucharistic theology. In doing so, they reflected their understanding that these two aspects of a sacrament—its lived expression in prayer and its doctrinal expression in theology— are closely related. The national statement notes that "in addition to the growing harmony in ways of thinking about eucharistic sacrifice, there is a significant convergence in the actual practice of eucharistic worship." The international statement reminds us that "the concrete shape of the liturgy had a special place in our considerations, because the eucharistic reality embraces doctrine and life, confession and liturgical form, piety and practice."

It is important to emphasize the significance of the recent liturgical changes in both churches because such changes influence each Church's understanding of the Eucharist. One major difficulty with previous Lutheran and Roman Catholic discussions was that they focused only on the real presence of Christ in the Eucharist and on the Eucharist as sacrifice. At the time of the Reformation, these two concepts controlled and dominated eucharistic understanding. Those emphases were also reflected in the liturgy. Popular piety centered on the "moment of consecration," the moment when the real presence would actually "begin." The emphasis on presence and sacrifice also influenced the conception of the ordained minister's role. In Roman Catholic worship, the priest spoke the words "This is my body; this is my blood" much more slowly and distinctly than the rest of the prayers in the canon. The gestures of elevation and genuflection also emphasized the idea of the real presence. Luther retained that understanding when he stripped the Canon but left the formula of consecration intact. He also indicated his position on the Eucharist as sacrifice by eliminating most sacrificial terms from the liturgy.

"Separating the Inseparable"

On the basis of a review of Luther's reform of the Roman canon and his attempt to construct a eucharistic theology, we must say that many highly questionable assumptions of sixteenth-century liturgical experience provided the basis for later Roman Catholic and Protestant understandings of the Eucharist. One example is a theology of the Eucharist in which an "either/or" approach became the focal point for discussions concerning law and Gospel, sacrifice and sacrament. It is now commonly agreed that both the Lutheran and the Roman Catholic traditions "separated the inseparable" in such discussions. That is to say, they separated and isolated the understanding of the real presence of Jesus Christ in the Eucharist from discussions of the Eucharist as sacrifice. But real presence and sacrifice should not be separated because they are found together in the prayers of the liturgy. In fact, their full comprehension requires that they be united. Other separations divorced the real presence from the Eucharist as a communal action; that is, a division was made between presence and the use of the sacrament. Other theological cleavages separated sign and reality, subjective and objective, spiritual and physical, involvement and reception. Such separations severely harmed the understanding of the sacramental unity of the Eucharist. A sacrament involves a reality that is made real in signs, an objective presence requiring the involvement of the community's subjective dispositions, a physical reality that is also a spiritual gift. Above all, the Eucharist is a sacrament that requires the possibility of receiving the elements at the same time as it demands personal involvement throughout the celebration.

Although some of the separations mentioned above tend to caricature former Roman Catholic and Lutheran explanations of the Eucharist, contemporary liturgical reform reunites what was separated, at least in the popular mind. The liturgy and the texts of the eucharistic prayers, taken in their fullness, can serve as a refreshing, theologically sound foundation for developing a more complete eucharistic theology. In this way, presence and sacrifice, certainly the clearest of theological difficulties existing between Lutherans and Roman Catholics, will become part of a larger picture. These two aspects will be seen to have meaning on levels of understanding usually not explored in eucharistic theology. The unity of the liturgy will form a solid basis for a unified theology. Among other things, liturgical and theological unity requires that the Eucharist be carefully understood as a liturgical action, as a communal action, as a symbolic action, and as a ritualized meal. This approach unites aspects of eucharistic theology that have long been neglected in both Roman Catholic and Lutheran treatments of the sacrament.

A review of the eucharistic prayers in the present liturgies of both churches can help bring out aspects of the sacrament that have long been neglected in theology and popular piety. Those aspects have influenced the joint statements of both the national and international dialogues. Most importantly, the contemporary liturgies have caused the two traditions to move beyond their limited understandings in which eucharistic presence and eucharistic sacrifice were separated. An examination of the liturgy can aid ecumenical discussions at the local level because the ground and source for such dialogues will be the Church's prayer which has already become familiar because of repeated use and, it is hoped, greater understanding.

What the Church Does at the Eucharist

The basis for discussions of the Eucharist is neither presence nor sacrifice, but what the Church does at worship. Because Roman Catholics and Lutherans have been concerned to affirm or restate positions about particular aspects of the Eucharist, they have not explored very well how the Eucharist is related to the historical and risen life of Jesus Christ. In the Eucharist, Christians make a memorial of the past deeds of Jesus Christ. Thereby the Church enters once again into his saving life, death, and resurrection. Much more is involved than mere human thought about those deeds of Jesus Christ. An actualization of those saving deeds occurs in and through the liturgical celebration.

Examining the new Roman Catholic and Lutheran eucharistic prayers, we note how that mysterious occurrence is expressed:

> Father, calling to mind the death your Son endured for our sal-
> vation,
> his glorious resurrection and ascension into heaven,
> and ready to greet him when he comes again,
> we offer you in thanksgiving this holy and living sacrifice.
>
> (Roman Catholic Eucharistic Prayer III)

> Father, we now celebrate this memorial of our redemption.
> We recall Christ's death, his descent among the dead,
> his resurrection, and his ascension to your right hand;
> and, looking forward to his coming in glory,
> we offer you his body and blood, the acceptable sacrifice
> which brings salvation to the whole world.
>
> (Roman Catholic Eucharistic Prayer IV)

> Therefore, gracious Father,
> with this bread and cup
> we remember the life
> our Lord offered for us.
> And believing the witness
> of his resurrection
> we await his coming in power
> to share with us
> the great and promised feast.
>
> (*Lutheran Book of Worship,* Holy Communion, #31).

> Therefore, O God,
> with this bread and cup
> we remember the incarnation of your Son:
> his human birth
> and the covenant he made with us.
> We remember the sacrifice of his life:
> his eating with outcasts,
> and his acceptance of death.
> But chiefly (on this day)
> we remember his rising from the tomb,

his ascension to the seat of power,
and his sending of the holy and life-giving Spirit.
We cry out for the resurrection of our lives,
when Christ will come again
in beauty and power
to share with us the great and promised feast.

(*Lutheran Book of Worship,*
Ministers' Edition, Alternate Prayer).

These texts show the concern of the two churches to unite the present experience of the liturgy with the entire life of Christ. The free gift of Christ's life for us and our present share in that life are the two focal points of these "memorial" prayers. A great advantage of these texts lies in their insistence that the present action of the Church is related to the past and present deeds of Christ. Because these new texts are now available, there are also other areas that can be discussed further by Lutherans and Roman Catholics in an attempt to clarify their understanding of the Eucharist.

In some Roman Catholic theological treatments, it is common to associate the Eucharist almost exclusively with the passion and death of Jesus Christ. The Eucharist has been called the "unbloody sacrifice of the cross," a phrase that clearly limits the association of the Eucharist with the risen life of Christ. Roman Catholics must ask themselves how they now understand the Eucharist inasmuch as the texts of their eucharistic prayer speak about the earthly life, the passion, the death, and the resurrection of Jesus Christ. It is no longer sufficient to isolate the Eucharist and associate it with the events of Calvary alone. On the Lutheran side, there is the question of how to understand the action of the Church at the Eucharist. To "make the memorial" of Jesus Christ in the liturgy implies something objective and real. "Memorial" means something far more than mere subjective recollection. The reality of the memorial needs to be underscored in a way that reflects the new liturgical texts.

In addition, once it becomes clear what the Church *does* in the Eucharist, then the idea of presence and the use of the sacrament must also conform to the new understanding. This means that, above all, the Eucharist must be seen as an *action* of the Church. Sacraments are not things, but divine and human *actions* in which people participate. Both Roman Catholics and Lutherans can profit from this more dynamic concept of a sacrament because both have previously encouraged passivity in worship. The full liturgical reality requires the engagement and involvement of worshipers in a lived experience.

The Eucharist as the Work of the Holy Spirit

A renewed emphasis on the prayer invoking the Holy Spirit is another significant development in both Lutheran and Roman Catholic liturgies. That prayer reflects the inherent tension that exists between the acts of the celebrating community and the primary action of the Holy Spirit in worship. In their revised liturgies, both traditions have clearly affirmed that the mystery and energy of the Eucharist must be sought in prayer.

Father, may this Holy Spirit sanctify these offerings.
Let them become the body and blood of Jesus Christ our Lord
as we celebrate the great mystery
which he left us as an everlasting covenant.

Lord, look upon this sacrifice which you have given to your
   Church;
and, by your Holy Spirit, gather all who share this bread and
   wine
into the one body of Christ, a living sacrifice of praise.
                    (Roman Catholic Eucharistic Prayer IV).

Send now, we pray,
your Holy Spirit,
the Spirit of our Lord
and of his resurrection,
that we who receive
the Lord's body and blood
may live to the praise
of your glory
and receive our inheritance
with all your saints in light

                              (*Lutheran Book of Worship,*
                              Holy Communion, #31)

Send now, we pray,
your Holy Spirit,
that we and all who share in this bread and cup
may be united in the fellowship of the Holy Spirit,
may enter the fullness of the kingdom of heaven,
and may receive our inheritance with all your saints in light.

(Luthern Book of Worship,
Ministers' Edition, Alternate Prayer).

The recognition of the Holy Spirit's role will influence how the worshiping community views human initiatives. Sometimes Roman Catholics have emphasized the priest's "power to consecrate" to such a degree that little remained for the congregation to do in liturgy. More unsettling was the fact that God's initiative in worship was frequently forgotten. Because of their new eucharistic prayers, Roman Catholics will have to re-examine their understanding of the priest's role. The involvement of the congregation in worship is not something optional or extra. Rather, the faith of the community and the active engagement of the community in worship are essential for any priestly act in the Eucharist. The priest functions by virtue of the already existing faith of the community. Priestly actions make sense only in that context. Further, the faith and action of both priest and people ultimately depend on God's initiative. That initiative is expressed in the action of the Holy Spirit. The new prayers thus reflect a richer understanding of the Eucharist and should be studied thoroughly, especially by Roman Catholics.

From a Lutheran perspective, the use of prayers invoking the Holy Spirit is a marked improvement over the older rites which contained only a recounting of the events at the Last Supper. A fuller theology of the Eucharist is possible when the Holy Spirit's initiative is recalled and emphasized. The Holy Spirit is present and active throughout the entire liturgy, not just at the moment of consecration. This realization can be helpful for developing the spirituality of Lutheran congregations. The doctrinal teaching about "Christ alone" will be enhanced by such emphasis on the Holy Spirit, because only in the power of the Holy Spirit does the Church share in the life of Jesus Christ present in the Eucharist.

From Past and Present to Future

For both Lutherans and Roman Catholics, every liturgical celebration in the present refers back to the deeds of Jesus Christ, specifically the events of the Last Supper. However, the Eucharist involves much more than a backward look. Liturgy also refers to the future when the sacraments will give way to the everlasting banquet in the kingdom of heaven. While Jesus Christ is certainly present and active in the Eucharist now, the Church nonetheless longs for the day when the Lord will be seen face-to-face in God's kingdom. Indeed, those will be blessed who are called to the supper of the lamb of God (Rev. 19:9). Until that time, the pilgrim Church shares in the Eucharist, which is a sign of that heavenly banquet.

In theology, there has been a revival of the concept of the Eucharist as a sacramental realization of the new covenant in Jesus Christ and as the community's share in the yet-to-be-realized kingdom of God. The history of eucharistic theology has not always reflected these aspects of the Eucharist as a provisional reality. The Reformation controversies were of no help in reviving such a concept. In the contemporary reform of Lutheran and Roman Catholic worship, those deficiencies of the past have been remedied. There are clear references to the promised feast of the kingdom in the eucharistic prayers and acclamations. This can be seen in the Roman Catholic acclamations:

Christ has died,
Christ is risen,
Christ will come again.

Dying you destroyed our death;
rising you restored our life.
Lord Jesus, come in glory.

When we eat this bread and drink this cup,
we proclaim your death, Lord Jesus,
until you come in glory.

It is also clear in the Lutheran acclamations:

Christ has died,
Christ is risen,
Christ will come again.

Amen. Come, Lord Jesus.

Amen. Come, Holy Spirit.

While it is commonly understood that Lutherans and Roman Catholics have held a belief in the real presence of Jesus Christ, now it is also clear that they realize that in the Eucharist the Church is able to span the past and future through Jesus Christ who is both present and yet to come. Such an emphasis in no way diminishes the reality of Christ's presence in the sacrament. What it provides, however, is an understanding that the full revelation of Jesus Christ will be realized when believers have passed from the present life to the promised life of heavenly glory. With such an orientation, believers can understand that the Eucharist also points to the yet-to-be-revealed presence of Christ in the kingdom. A hymn widely used by both traditions states this teaching precisely:

So, Lord, at length when sacraments shall cease,
May we be one with all your Church above—
One with your saints in one unbroken peace;
One as your bride in one unbounded love;
More blessed still, in peace and love to be
One with the Trinity in unity.
                (*Lutheran Book of Worship,* Hymn #206, st. 4)

In their continued use of the eucharistic prayers, local congregations can gain a deeper awareness of the theology and spirituality of the sacrament. In light of the great similarities which now exist in the forms of their prayers, it is not surprising that Roman Catholics and Lutherans have renewed confidence in their ability to speak to one another about the Eucharist with greater understanding and fuller agreement.

Church Teaching on the Presence

In addition to the liturgy, another factor that can aid ecumenical dialogue on the Eucharist lies in the fact that both churches have always shared a common interest in preserving the faith by means of doctrinal formulations. The Lutheran confessional books, as well as the decrees and documents of the Council of Trent and the Second Vatican Council, are ample witnesses to that concern. Clearly, both churches share a rich theological tradition which helps specify areas of agreement and divergence. Both share a common heritage from the sixteenth century in eucharistic teaching as well as in worship. Theologically, the major concern of that era was to clarify what each party taught about the presence of Christ in the Eucharist and about the sacrificial nature of the Eucharist. Most often those statements were composed in light of and in opposition to the doctrinal teaching of the other party.

As a result of the controversies that occurred before and during the sixteenth century, the Roman Catholic Church wished to affirm both the reality of Christ's presence in the Eucharist and the sacrificial nature of the Eucharist. The language used was very precise and highly technical. The term "transubstantiation" was used in reference to the real presence, and the sacrificial dimension was stated in the same kind of language. From a Roman Catholic viewpoint, the intention was to protect those aspects of the Eucharist from being neglected or forgotten. From the Lutheran perspective, the term "transubstantiation" was unacceptable because it seemed too rationalistic. Lutherans preferred the term "sacramental union" to describe the relationship between bread and wine and Christ's body and blood.

It is no surprise that the participants in the contemporary Lutheran-Roman Catholic dialogue were interested in treating the two traditional aspects of eucharistic theology. The national statement has only two sections: "The Eucharist as Sacrifice" and "The Presence of Christ in the Lord's Supper." The same topics are found in the international agreement, but the context of the discussion is somewhat wider and more comprehensive. In the international statement, eucharistic presence and sacrifice are treated in the first part of the text under "Joint Witness," but the different ways in which the churches affirm these concepts is considered under "Common Tasks."

Because of the common history which underlies those topics, the two churches found that ecumenical dialogue was relatively easy. What helped the dialogue was a realization that both traditions have gone beyond their sixteenth-century positions. That realization helped to move the discussion from a concentration on past controversies to an examination of present agreements. Faced with the task of considering eucharistic presence, the dialogue participants began to realize that they had to avoid slogans, and caricatures of one another's theological positions. They had to move beyond mere repetition of language found in past theological statements of the churches and uncover the meaning behind those cherished church teachings.

Two of the position papers prepared for discussion by participants in the national dialogue were careful studies of the theological climate which was responsible for use of the term "transubstantiation." In their final statement the participants noted: "Today . . . when Lutheran theologians read contemporary Catholic expositions, it becomes clear to them that the dogma of transubstantiation intends to affirm the fact of Christ's presence and of the change which takes place, and is not an attempt to explain *how* Christ becomes present." As a result of the dialogue, a more complete understanding of the term was achieved. Both Roman Catholics and Lutherans have begun to appreciate why the term came into use. Although Lutherans still prefer to avoid the word because of its historical associations, they have begun to recognize its intent and meaning more fully. Both Lutherans and Roman Catholics clearly affirm their faith in the real presence of Jesus Christ in the Eucharist. An appreciation of the various terms that have been used to assert that belief has also emerged from the dialogue. The participants maintained "that no single vocabulary or conceptual framework can be adequate, exclusive or final in this theological enterprise."

One lesson of the dialogue is that church members must move beyond "pat" definitions and caricatures when discussing the Eucharist. Roman Catholics have often caricatured Reformation thought by insisting that Protestants understand the Eucharist in a "merely symbolic" way. Lutherans avoided using the term "transubstantiation" because they said it was too "rationalistic," a caricature of Roman Catholic theology. The dialogue emphasized the need for members of both traditions to understand the highly symbolic character of the sacraments and to express their faith in the Eucharist through contemporary language.

Teachings about Sacrifice

Progress has also been made in discussions of the Eucharist as sacrifice. Both churches now "agree that the celebration of the Eucharist is the Church's sacrifice of praise and self-offering or oblation." Further, both affirm that Christ's sacrifice cannot be repeated and that the Eucharist has its foundation in that unique event. Lutherans avoided using the word "sacrifice" when referring to the Eucharist because they feared that the term would obscure the importance of the one, unique sacrifice of Jesus Christ.

In the national dialogue, the participants on each side began to understand sacrifice in a different way than before. Each side reinterpreted its own positions in that light. On the Roman Catholic side, this meant understanding that the sacrifice of the cross is unrepeatable and that an essential unity exists between eucharistic worship and the one sacrifice of Jesus Christ. Contemporary Roman Catholic explanations of the way in which the Church "offers Christ" in the Eucharist have helped Lutherans clarify the relationship between the Eucharist and the unrepeatable sacrifice of Jesus Christ. In the sacrament "the members of the body of Christ are united through Christ with God and with one another in such a way that they become participants in his worship, his self-offering, his sacrifice to the Father. Through this union between Christ and Christians, the eucharistic assembly 'offers Christ' by consenting in the power of the Holy Spirit to be offered by him to the Father." From a Lutheran perspective, the discussion of sacrifice meant being more precise and less argumentative about "private" Masses because some of the arguments used against "private" Masses have caricatured Roman Catholic theology.

Similar progress in nuancing theological positions can be seen in the international statement which speaks about the need for everyone to be better informed about the doctrinal positions of both churches. The statement notes that "in ecumenical discussion we have learned better to understand each other's interpretations. Research into the historical background of the Reformation polemic as well as the consideration of new developments in both churches has proved especially helpful. Increasingly we recognize the interpretations of the other as a challenge to our own position and as a help in improving, deepening, and enlivening it." This is certainly an impressive statement by members of churches that have been known more for their controversy and polemic about sacrifice than for their common understanding of one another.

To continue the dialogue on the Eucharist we must speak about presence and sacrifice together. An emphasis on the presence of Christ is limited if a theology of presence does not lead to considerations of Communion. An emphasis on sacrifice is imprecise if it does not reveal the fact that through the Eucharist contemporary believers are made sharers in the paschal mystery of Christ. One participates in the Eucharist for the purpose of Communion and sanctification in community. One does not worship in order merely to observe the presence of Christ or to think about his death and resurrection in the past. This approach requires that the Eucharist be appreciated as a highly symbolic action that totally involves and engages the congregation. Also necessary is the understanding that eucharistic theology must be expressed in less dogmatic, more dynamic, more personally-oriented language.

A very useful approach for local congregations is one that helps them to see the relationship which should exist between various forms of prayer and the theology of the Eucharist. Local communities can study liturgical prayers to see how they help "flesh out" the meaning of Christ's presence in the Eucharist. Local communities can consider scriptural and liturgical texts which deal with offering oneself as a sacrifice and learn that they complement their understanding of the sacrifice of Christ present in the Eucharist. Attention will thus shift toward an appreciation of the Eucharist as a dynamic event, an action that has great influence on the Church's doctrinal teaching.

Further Dialogue and Practical Changes

In the course of the dialogue, it will probably become apparent that some matters remain unresolved between Lutherans and Roman Catholics. These differences should not cause pessimism, because the grounds of agreement are far broader and wider than they have been at any time since the Reformation. The remaining differences should be noted honestly and fairly. A discussion can be helpful that centers not only on obvious differences in practice, but also on the factors that lie behind those differences. Such differences may actually be agreements whose concrete expressions are somewhat divergent. Liturgical practices vary from community to community. Thus local dialogue in the area of liturgical practice will be even more important for the clarification of differences.

Frequency of the Eucharist

For Roman Catholics the celebration of the Eucharist on Sunday is normative. Daily celebrations are also commonplace and attest to a strong eucharistic orientation. Such a practice cannot so easily be assumed to exist among Lutherans. While the Roman Catholic Church has widely accepted the Reformation focus on the liturgy of the Word, many Lutheran congregations still celebrate only a service of the Word weekly, and the Eucharist less often. From the viewpoint of early Christian tradition, Lutheran congregations need to re-evaluate their expectations concerning eucharistic worship. The Lord's day celebrated without the Lord's Supper is something unthinkable for Roman Catholics. That it is indeed thinkable for many Lutherans should arouse serious reflection and evaluation on their part. Local ecumenical dialogue can confront this difference in practice and give the participants an opportunity to consider the reasons for their participation in worship and how often they should do so.

Private Masses

Although weekly, even daily, eucharistic celebration is a Roman Catholic expectation, there lingers among Catholics a certain "clericalism" with regard to worship. An example of this clericalism is the so-called "private" Masses celebrated by priests who are not needed for ministry at a particular time by their communities. Indeed, the sixteenth-century problem of "Mass priests" who abused their privilege of eucharistic celebration has ceased. However, the practice of celebrating "private" Masses still continues in some places, even though less frequently than before. Local dialogue groups should examine this practice and determine what they can learn from it about theoretical agreement being mitigated by actual practice.

Liturgical Experiences, Not Teaching

There was a good deal of individualism in the piety of the sixteenth century. Moreover, a "high" concept of the Eucharist influenced the way in which the Church spoke about the sacrament. Although Lutheran efforts since that time have borne fruit in making the Eucharist more intelligible, many Lutheran pastors, while good teachers, are poor leaders of prayer. The same situation plagues Roman Catholics because the liturgy has been considered a matter of forms and rites to be performed. Leaders of public prayer have become teachers or observers of rubrics. In this era of liturgical revision, ministers of both churches must go beyond mere texts, rites and forms in an effort to foster prayer and an experience of God's presence among the community. Lutheran pastors and communities can evaluate how well their services promote such an experience. Roman Catholics can inquire whether their liturgy leads to true fellowship and devotion. The liturgical reforms of both churches are intended to foster such liturgical experiences of the living God among his people.

Preaching the Word

Lutherans have a distinct advantage over Roman Catholics because they have a greater appreciation of preaching God's Word. Although Roman Catholics have recently revised the cycle of scriptural readings used at Mass, they still need opportunities to share their experiences and hopes about the homily or sermon. While definite reforms have already taken place in the ministry of preaching among Roman Catholics, they can gain great insight into the importance of preaching from Lutherans. In local ecumenical dialogues, questions can deal with how well preaching leads to the Eucharist and how effectively the message relates to the community's daily life. Lutherans might also review their own expectations about preaching. Do they wish merely to learn something, or do they desire to enter more fully into the mystery of Christ revealed to them in preaching and proclaiming the Word?

Sacraments and Things

A sacrament is intended to enable personal encounter with the Lord. Sacraments are not things primarily; they are saving events. It would be interesting to discover how the concept of sacraments as things will surface in local discussions. When we speak about "receiving" the Eucharist or "taking" Holy Communion, we betray a mechanical understanding of the sacrament. Sacraments should be understood as encounters between God and his people. Sacraments require human activity, participation and faith. Local dialogues can help in this discussion if the participants gain a more dynamic appreciation of the Eucharist and realize that Lutherans and Roman Catholics have moved away from their older understanding of the sacraments as a result of the recent reforms in liturgy.

Church Sacraments

Another benefit from local discussions of the Eucharist may be most significant from the viewpoint of sacramental theology. Formerly, Lutherans and Roman Catholics devoted great attention to the ways in which the individual benefits from a sacrament. The individualism of the late Middle Ages has not disappeared in either church. Despite the recent reforms, one of the more difficult things to achieve has been a communal understanding of sacraments. Local dialogues can raise this question frankly and ask whether people celebrate sacraments only for themselves and their own benefit, or whether they view their personal participation in relation to the community's experience. Both communities will have to examine how well they see liturgy as existing for the entire community, not for individuals alone.

For Roman Catholics this communal understanding of the Eucharist was forcefully reflected in the recent controversy concerning the "sign of peace." When that gesture was restored to its original setting in the Eucharist, there was much consternation among some local communities. More than a mere gesture was at stake. To give the sign of peace to others implied that individuals had a communal understanding of the Eucharist. Some discussion of this gesture and its full meaning can be very enlightening for local communities. There is more than a mere degree of difference between the Eucharist as a celebration for the whole community and the Eucharist as my private share in a public ceremony.

The joint statements of 1967 and 1978 provide ample evidence that a new age has begun for Lutherans and Roman Catholics who can now speak with unanimity about an impressive number of issues in eucharistic theology. Much work remains to be done. Not only must we continue along the way of establishing wider agreement, but also people at all levels of church life must be encouraged to experience and discuss such agreements. Although no ecumenical statement on the Eucharist can be regarded as definitive at this point, every document of consensus helps the partners to grow in unity and to see that truth resides not in a self-serving theology, but in a theology predicated on dialogue and exchange across denominational lines.

FOR STUDY AND DISCUSSION

1. What were some of the characteristics of the Roman Catholic Mass as it was usually celebrated just before the time of the Reformation? How did Martin Luther reform the Catholic liturgy?
2. How has the Roman Catholic Mass been changed as the result of the Second Vatican Council? Have there been similar changes in Lutheran worship?
3. What are the basic liturgical principles that motivated Lutherans and Roman Catholics to reform their styles of worship?
4. What implications for ecumenism can be drawn from the recent liturgical changes that have been made in both churches?
5. How do recent liturgical reforms reflect each church's current understanding of the Eucharist?
6. What is meant by the statement that "many highly questionable assumptions of sixteenth-century liturgical experience provided the basis for later Roman Catholic and Protestant understandings of the Eucharist"? Give an example of such a theology of the Eucharist.
7. What is the basic starting point for discussions of eucharistic theology among Lutherans and Roman Catholics today? How is such a discussion reflected in the new liturgical texts of each tradition?
8. How is the Eucharist related to the work of the Holy Spirit? How have Lutherans and Roman Catholics changed their positions regarding that relationship?
9. How is the present celebration of the Eucharist linked with both the past events of Jesus' life and the kingdom of God that is yet to come?
10. What does the Roman Catholic Church teach concerning the presence of Jesus Christ in the Eucharist? What is the Lutheran

teaching, and how does it differ, if it does, from the Roman Catholic teaching?

11. How have Lutherans and Roman Catholics in dialogue made progress in regard to their understanding of the Eucharist as sacrifice? What must Lutherans and Roman Catholics do to achieve further understanding on this subject?

12. What are some of the differences which still must be resolved by Lutherans and Roman Catholics regarding eucharistic teaching and practice? What are some ways in which each difference may be resolved concretely?

FOR FURTHER READING

Leonard Swidler, ed., *The Eucharist in Ecumenical Dialogue* (New York: Paulist Press).

Modern Eucharistic Agreement (London: SPCK).

One Baptism, One Eucharist and a Mutually Recognized Ministry (Lausanne: World Council of Churches).

John Krump, *What a Modern Catholic Believes about the Eucharist* (Chicago: Thomas More Press).

Ernest Koenker, *Worship in Word and Sacrament* (St. Louis: Condordia Publishing House).

Gordon Lathrop, *The Hungry Feast: Reflections on a Lutheran Theology of Worship* (New York: Lutheran Forum Cassettes).

Paul C. Empie and T. Austin Murphy, eds., *Lutherans and Catholics in Dialogue I-IV* (Minneapolis: Augsburg Publishing House).

4. The Ministry of the Church

"As the Father has sent me, even so I send you. Receive the Holy Spirit. If you forgive the sins of any, they are forgiven; if you retain the sins of any, they are retained." Those words of Jesus from the Gospel of John have traditionally been viewed by Roman Catholics and Lutherans as authorizing a "special" ministry in the Church. While members of the two groups have often disagreed on what that ministry is and does, both have always maintained a ministerial "office" or "order" within the larger body of Christians.

"I believe in one, holy, catholic and apostolic Church." When both Lutherans and Roman Catholics unite to offer worship, we recite that phrase of the Creed. For members of both communions, there exists one Church, holy in its being called apart and sanctified by God, catholic in its universality through time and place, and apostolic in its faithfulness to the Church's original foundation. However, we have often disagreed about the details of that Church's structure and historical manifestations.

These basic understandings have not prevented us from some confusion in the use of the terms "church" and "ministry." We often confuse even those in our own tradition because we use these words with different definitions and emphases. In modern English the word "church," for example, is used to name an individual denomination, a building for worship, and even a religious service, as in the sentence, "We're going to church." Yet all of us know that there is a far deeper meaning which "church" denotes. The same is true for "ministry." We talk about a priest or pastor as a minister and about the work of the clergy as the Church's "ministry." Yet we also see reference to a "ministry" of all members of the Church, a ministry expressed through their daily vocations in home, factory, office and field.

Let's try to see in what ways Roman Catholics and Lutherans agree on the deepest definitions of Church and ministry. Then we will be able to discuss those issues about which we disagree. While we agree on definitions of the Church and its ministry, we differ in our definitions of the specialized ministry of the ordained. This difference affects our dealings with one another in important ways.

A Church of Faithful People

The Augsburg Confession calls the Church "the assembly of all believers among whom the Gospel is preached in its purity and the holy sacraments are administered according to the Gospel" (Art. VII). Thus, the Church is people gathered around word and sacraments, "the assembly of all believers and saints" (Art. VIII), created by the grace of baptism and sustained by the grace of the Eucharist. The Lutheran document, partly in reaction to certain dominant cultural patterns of the Middle Ages, stressed the importance of each individual Christian as a member of the Church. Each person within the Church finds equal forgiveness and grace through baptism into Christ. Additional church commitments, such as monastic vows and voluntary disciplines, cannot create a second, higher class of Christians, from the Lutheran viewpoint, because the grace of baptism makes the Church "the assembly of all believers and saints."

One need hardly have paid much attention to the events and documents of the Second Vatican Council to know that perhaps its most famous phrase was "the people of God." The Church is not the hierarchy, the councils or the buildings. The Church is the people of God. In the *Dogmatic Constitution on the Church,* chapter one provides a stunning list of biblical images to elaborate this phrase. The Church is "the kingdom of Christ now present in mystery," "one body in Christ," "a people made one with the unity of the Father, the Son, and the Holy Spirit." The Church is a sheepfold, a piece of farm land, the edifice of God, our mother, the spouse of Christ, the community of faith, hope and charity. The second chapter particularly describes the people of God. All baptized Christians who are not Roman Catholics are recognized as being linked in some way with Roman Catholics in the one Church (n.15). The second chapter concludes with the prayer that all the world "may become the people of God, the body of the Lord, and the temple of the Holy Spirit."

Although more than four hundred years and many theological quarrels separated the Augsburg Confession and the documents of the Second Vatican Council, the emphasis, as shown on the terms the assembly of believers and the people of God, is the same—that the Church is every baptized person. We see the same agreement in the definition of ministry. The Augsburg Confession emphasized that each baptized person lives out the ministry of God, urging that "everyone, each according to his own calling, manifest Christian love and genuine good works in his station of life" (Art. XVI). The Reformation's position that the laity is equal to the clergy in God's sight can be seen in the Augsburg Confession's complaints about the preferential status of monks and in its recommendation that the laity be allowed to receive communion in both kinds, bread and wine.

A strong emphasis on the ministry of the laity is seen in the Second Vatican Council's *Decree on the Apostolate of the Laity.* For example, we read: "The laity, too, share in the priestly, prophetic and royal office of Christ and therefore have their own role to play in the mission of the whole people of God in the Church and in the world" (Ch. I), and again: "The right and duty to exercise the apostolate is common to all the faithful, both clergy and laity, and the laity also have their own proper roles in building up the Church" (Ch. V). This decree discusses at length the role of the laity's ministry both in parish life and in secular vocations.

The recent Lutheran-Roman Catholic dialogues repeat this essential agreement on the ministry of the laity. The common statement regarding "Eucharist and Ministry" asserts:

> The Church has, then, the task of proclaiming the Gospel to all, believers and unbelievers. This task or service of the whole Church is spoken of as "ministry." . . . We recognize therefore that the whole Church has a priesthood in Christ, i.e., a ministry or service from God to men. . . . The special ministry [of the ordained] must not be discussed in isolation but in context of the ministry of the whole people of God. . . . All who are united

with Jesus as Christ and Lord by baptism and faith are also united with, and share, his priesthood (*Dialogues,* Vol. IV, p. 9).

The documents of the Second Vatican Council also emphasized many ways in which laity and clergy share a common life. The word "ministry" is repeatedly used in discussing the lay life of all God's people. The laity also take part in the apostolic mission, not only in the witness of their daily lives, but also in their constant opportunities to give verbal witness for Christ. In the liturgy, the laity participate with the clergy in offering spiritual sacrifices; all the people, not solely the priest, offer worship to God. Although in the past there has sometimes been too great a gulf between clergy and laity, the documents say that "what they share in common is far more fundamental, far more extensive, and far more decisive that the distinction between them" (*Dialogues,* Vol. IV, p. 205). There is, surely, a diversity of service, but more importantly there is a unity of purpose.

This unity of purpose is the baptized life. The Gospel of Mark speaks about Jesus' commissioned life as a servant of God beginning at his baptism. Our baptism incorporates us into Christ and commissions us to minister before God as God's children. Around 200 A.D., Hippolytus wrote a great eucharistic prayer in which thanks is given that we can stand before God and "minister as priests" to God. This prayer is included in the minister's edition of the new *Lutheran Book of Worship* and is recalled in the second eucharistic prayer of the *Roman Missal.* We stand in God's presence serving as a "priestly people" when we present our prayers to God, when we offer our lives in praise, when we live out our days as if each thing we do is a gift of thanks to the Lord. As God's priests we also forgive one another and thus speak the Gospel of Christ in the world.

Roman Catholics and Lutherans thus agree on the essential definitions of Church and ministry. The Church is the people of God and the assembly of believers. The ministry of the Church is lived out by all baptized members in their lives, their daily vocations and their parish interaction. Furthermore, we willingly recognize each other as members of the Church. How different this is from days gone by. Far too often in the past, both Lutherans and Roman Catholics have described themselves in terms which implied condemnations of the other. Current agreements on such important expressions as "the ministry of the Church" show that we can now go beyond the worst of such name-calling.

Different Terms, Different Understandings?

When we define the specialized ministry, however, differences arise. These differences unfortunately seem quite significant and stand in the way of our attempts to worship together. The precise meaning of ordination is disputed, and this dispute is expressed in such controverted issues as apostolic succession and women's ordination. The Lutheran-Roman Catholic dialogues have shown, however, that both groups view these issues in a different way than they did in the sixteenth century. Let's look at these issues to see whether, while moving along separately, we are also moving toward one another.

Some of us use words like priest, pastor, presbyter, bishop, deacon, and minister to describe Church order. In order not to misunderstand one another, let us review what these words mean and how we use them. The word "priest" comes originally from the Greek word *presbyteros,* an elder in the religious community. The New Testament does not use the term "priest" of Church leaders, but the Church's later use of the word recalls the priesthood in Old Testament times. Although God's people saw that each person shares a priesthood before God, with the power and right to approach God with offerings of praise and prayers of submission, some of the Hebrew people were appointed by God to be in special charge of public worship. These levitical priests functioned in the temple to consult God concerning his will, to teach and to offer sacrifice. This last responsibility is perhaps the one we know best. Many religions use the word "priest" to name the one who offers sacrifice to a deity. Today, Roman Catholics use the word "priest" to name those who are ordained especially to preside at the Eucharist. Priests can function in quite different roles, in or out of the parish, as pastors, teachers, poets or factory workers, but all Roman Catholic priests can lead the people of God in public worship.

The word "pastor" comes from the Latin verb meaning "to feed," and it emphasizes the shepherding role of a leader in the Christian community. A pastor is one who tends God's sheep, caring for them, feeding them, and protecting them from harm. Lutherans use the word "pastor" more than any other to name their ordained clergy, and it is significant that the word recalls tending, rather than offering. Roman Catholics use the word "pastor" to specify the head of a large parish, the priest who cares even for the other priests there.

The word "presbyter" is an exact transliteration of the Greek New Testament word *presbyteros.* The word had previously been used to describe a group of influential men in a Jewish synagogue, and it is the word which Scripture uses to name the elders in the first Christian communities. It is not clear in the New Testament what specific rights and responsibilities the presbyters had. Did they, for example, preside at the Eucharist? Were they the only people allowed to preside? These questions are difficult to answer conclusively from the New Testament data alone. It is safest to say that congregations in different places developed different patterns for leadership and different divisions of responsibility.

Varied Uses of "Bishop"

"Bishop" comes from the Greek word *episkopos,* and in its New Testament meaning it implies something like "overseer." It appears that in the early New Testament communities which were not exclusively Jewish and which therefore had no model such as the synagogue's elder, the office of the overseer developed. Again it is difficult to determine exactly what the *episkopos* oversaw and over what he had authority and responsibility. It seems clear that he functioned as a sole authority, rather than within a group of ruling elders as the *presbyteros* did. In current Roman Catholic usage, a bishop is the overseer of a diocese, the pastor of all its priests, a symbol of the powers given in Christ and held by all in the Church. As the chief minister, the bishop alone can ordinarily ordain clergy and confirm the faithful. By custom, numerous liturgical and ecclesiastical responsibilities also come his way as a primary figurehead in the Church.

Lutherans use the word "bishop" in two ways. That they usually call their clergy "pastors" and emphasize their function of overseeing is not completely an accident. It has sometimes been said that every Lutheran pastor is a bishop. When Roman Catholic bishops in many dioceses refused to ordain the dissenters at the time of the

Church's sixteenth-century rift, the Protestants claimed for the local clergy both the rights, and the rites, of a bishop. It often fell to parish clergy to ordain and confirm. The Church was described in terms of the local congregation, and thus the important role of the bishop was assumed by the parish pastor. In recent decades, however, many Lutherans in the United States have revived the use of the word "bishop" to describe the person previously called a synod or district president. (In Europe, the term bishop has been used by Lutherans all along.)

In the Roman Catholic Church there is also an order of deacons. At different times in history this order has had different roles. We know very little about what the deacon did in the early Church, but we do know that some of the early councils prescribed the rights of a deacon. Currently, the word is used in quite different ways. In some Lutheran parishes the deacon is a council member who takes the Sunday offering or oversees the building's maintenance. Several Christian groups are attempting to revive the order of deacon as a lay person's lifelong dedication to service within the Church. The Second Vatican Council described the diaconate as an ordination "not unto the priesthood, but unto a ministry of service." Different parish situations require that deacons be used differently. The best role for the permanent diaconate in the United States still must be discovered.

Ministers and Ministers

Because of these differences in the use of terms, the recent Lutheran-Roman Catholic dialogues decided to use the word "Minister" to designate the person who is ordained to the special "Ministry" of word and sacrament. The upper case "M" distinguished the ordained Minister from the lay minister, the baptized believer, whose ministry is expresed in daily living. This specialized Ministry within and for the Church was the focus of the fourth Lutheran-Roman Catholic series of dialogues on "Eucharist and Ministry." In both traditions, the validity of the eucharistic action is to some extent dependent on the person presiding over that action. Thus, in our conversations together the meaning and characteristics of the Minister must be considered.

The Lutheran-Roman Catholic dialogues have already expressed agreement on some essentials concerning the Ministry. It has a twofold task of proclaiming the Gospel to the world and of building up in Christ those who are belivers. The Minister stands with the people of God under Christ and also speaks to the people of God in the name of Christ. In both traditions, the Ministry is entered through ordination, although the precise understanding of ordination may differ. Both traditions see the Ministry as apostolic, although the precise understanding of how it is apostolic differs. Both Roman Catholic and Lutheran bibilical scholars agree that the development of Ministry in the New Testament Church is a complex matter which perhaps will never be completely resolved. New Testament texts offer different lists of special ministries in the Church, and it is never clear which ministers performed what tasks, or even if there was much consensus on this matter in the first centuries of the Christian era. While both Lutherans and Roman Catholics locate the roots of their ordained Ministry in the New Testament Church, most would now concede that it is impossible to do so in any literal sense.

The Apostolic Succession

One of the main obstacles to our communing together at one eucharistic table arises from the definition of the ordained Minister. In the Roman Catholic Church, a person competent to preside at the Eucharist must be a priest ordained by a bishop who himself is validly ordained. Thus, Roman Catholics do not consider Lutheran celebrations of communion as full and as complete as their own, because most Lutheran clergy have not been ordained by a bishop who is in the "apostolic succession."

Let us now look at what Roman Catholics mean by "apostolic succession." Already by 100 A.D., there was concern that the Christian doctrine taught and the liturgies conducted should be faithful to the Gospel. At that time, Ignatius of Antioch wrote: "Let no one do anything pertaining to the Church apart from the bishop." Ignatius wanted to insure the correct transmission of the Lord's teachings by allowing only those to teach, preach, baptize and preside at the liturgy who had been appointed by the bishop to do so. It is unclear whether the early theologians meant that an improperly trained or non-ordained person could not be authorized by the Church to do priestly things or whether they meant that such a person did not possess the special power which enabled those actions. In current Roman Catholic language, a sacrament is considered "invalid" if this requirement is not met.

We can document the claim that the Church has always maintained strict rulings concerning those who preside at the Eucharist. The Fourth Lateran Council in 1215 was one of the occasions when eucharistic celebrations unauthorized by a bishop were condemned. In response to the Reformation, the Roman Catholic Church at the Council of Trent in 1563 condemned the position that there could be legitimate Ministers of the word and sacraments apart from regular ordination by a bishop. The Council declared that those Ministers who stemmed from the Reformation were illegitimate. Yet, the Council did not go so far as to condemn the fact that during the Reformation ordinary parish priests, rather than bishops, had ordained some priests. The Second Vatican Council, however, made it clear that although a "defect" exists in those eucharistic celebrations over which an improperly-ordained Minister presides, nevertheless those celebrations still "commemorate the Lord's death and resurrection in the Holy Supper." The Second Vatican Council stated that an important aspect of the Eucharist is its relationship to the unity of the body of Christ which is symbolized by the Minister's unity with the local bishop, who in turn is in unity with the bishop of Rome. Needless to say, this also poses a problem for Eastern Orthodox Christians who are not in full communion with Rome.

An important factor in this Roman Catholic argument for the unity of the Church symbolized by the unity of the bishops is called "apostolic succession." This refers to the theory that there is a direct personal connection between each generation of bishops reaching from the apostles down to the present Pope and bishops. That is, one can list by name the successors to the apostles, and from this unbroken chain come all the legitimate bishops of every age and every land. According to this view, churches "in communion" with Rome must be able to trace their bishops directly back to the apostles in the same way as Rome does. Lutheranism's inability to do so, at least for the most part, therefore places a major obstacle in the way of improved Lutheran-Roman Catholic relations today. However, apostolic succession by itself does not secure the unity of bishops.

How a Term Developed

Who were the apostles? Until the nineteenth century it was common to speak about them as if they were, without doubt, the twelve disciples and Paul. More recent biblical studies of "apostle" show that the word meant somewhat different things to different writers. Luke and the Book of Acts seem to equate "apostle" with the twelve, while Paul uses "apostle" to mean a missionary who has seen the risen Lord. Paul describes himself as an "apostle," and he surely was not one of the twelve. In other parts of the New Testament, the word has slightly different casts of meaning. During the first century, Christian writers used "apostle" to refer to various aspects of Christian discipleship. For example, Justin Martyr (c. 165 A.D.) says that the apostles—the witnesses of the Lord's resurrection and the writers of the New Testament—were primarily links between Christ and the Church of present as well as future ages.

If these early writers identified the apostles in different ways, one cannot expect, at least this early, to have neat expositions of what apostolic succession meant. In 92 A.D., Clement of Rome was probably the first to write about the principle of succession. He says that the apostles personally ordained some men to the Ministry and ordered them to do likewise when the time came to choose their successors. During the second century, Irenaeus emphasized the idea that to determine which groups were true and faithful Christian communities, one must ascertain if their faith and practice is in harmony with the apostolic churches. Irenaeus was a conservative. He was convinced that it was necessary to check with those who remembered and lived the tradition of the past in order to be faithful in the present. These apostolic churches—and Irenaeus records a list of the important bishops in their historical order—provide the norms for other communities and are the authorities in any controverted issue of doctrine.

A further development of this principle arose in regard to questions of authority and jurisdiction. In those cases, properly-ordained bishops were said to be not merely in the succession of the apostles, but actually *the successors of* the apostles. Such a simple change in terms reflected a reinforcement of the conceptual relationship between the apostles and the bishops of a later age. In the matter of authority, then, the one who was considered to be correct in any controversy was the one who was legitimately a successor of the apostles.

By the fourth century this idea had developed somewhat. Augustine had to deal with a crisis in which people were asking if priests who were clearly unworthy of their office and were infamous for immoral lives were still able to preside validly over the Eucharist. By stating that the sacraments over which those priests presided were indeed valid, Augustine helped strengthen the growing conviction that when a priest was ordained by a bishop, he received a special, lifelong power which made his sacramental actions valid even though his life might belie his teachings. This judgment by Augustine also strengthened the idea of apostolic succession. There is an unbroken chain of authority descending from the apostles to the bishops and, through them, to the local priests which ensures the faithful transmission of the Gospel and the efficacious administration of the sacraments. Anyone performing sacramental functions outside the chain of succession is suspect, and such rites cannot be accepted as valid by the Catholic Church. Indeed, what demonstrates the Church's catholicity is its unity through the bishops as one universal body.

In our discussion, however, a point must also be made concerning the word "power." It was maintained that a priest who stands outside the apostolic succession does not have the "power" to preside validly over the Eucharist. A precise definition of "power" has never been achieved. Generally, it is thought to be power in the sense of capability. Thus, if a person who is not properly ordained should preside over the Eucharist, that Eucharist is defective because the person does not have the necessary power and is therefore incapable of performing the rite in its fullness. However, a second opinion defines power as authorization. In this understanding, no judgment is made about the effectiveness of the Eucharist among Lutherans. Instead such a Eucharist is said to be unauthorized, because the Lutheran pastor does not have authorization to function for the Church. While the first opinion is still more prevalent among Roman Catholics, the second, which is surely more open to ecumenical discussion, has never been officially criticized or condemned.

Reformation Views of Bishops

Historically in the Roman Catholic Church, there has been an interplay of two central issues involved with the "apostolic succession": (1) a concern for doctrinal integrity; (2) an identifiable chain of persons insuring the faith. We will now see what happened to this principle during the Reformation and what contemporary Lutherans have to say about it.

The Augsburg Confession attempted to achieve reconciliation. The Lutheran princes presented their common confession with a hope "to have all of us embrace and adhere to a single, true religion and live together in unity and one fellowship and Church, even as we are all enlisted under one Christ" (Preface). Thus, it would be mistaken to search the Augsburg Confession for a statement about Lutheran polity, a defense of the Lutheran way of ordering the Church, and, consequently, for some treatment of apostolic succession. In 1530 the Reformers had no intention of breaking from Rome. They wanted rather to make their theological points and to achieve what they considered were mandatory reforms. Although the Augsburg Confession has no section exclusively devoted to Church order, it does discuss at length what the Reformers contended were abuses of the episcopacy.

Article XXVIII, "The Power of Bishops," is significant in this regard. By showing how angry the Reformers were with some of their bishops, it helps us understand how future Protestants could envision a Church that existed apart from the succession of bishops. Some considerable distance had to be traveled by men like Martin Luther who began as loyal sons of Rome but who ended their days in a Church which they had helped to divide. In the Augsburg Confession, then, we hear the Reformers complaining that over the centuries the bishops had claimed far too much power. The Reformers asserted there was a justified, necessary, proper role for the bishop, and that role was to preach the Gospel, to forgive or retain sins, and to administer the sacraments. The power of bishops was effective only insofar as it was related to the Word and Sacrament. American Lutherans, chiefly because of historical circumstances related to their settling in North America, have a system which is less traditionally episcopal. The synod, a body composed of Ministers and congregations, does in fact serve in an episcopal role for many Lutherans. In 1530, however, the importance of bishops in relation to word and sacrament was not seriously questioned; thus some European Lutherans have a functioning episcopacy to this day.

During the Reformation, various privileges which had become the province of the bishop were vociferously condemned. Due in large part to a cultural situation in which the authorities of Church and state were either hopelessly entangled with one another or, indeed, were the very same people, some bishops had acquired great secular authority. The Reformers were highly critical of such enlarged powers of the bishops. A second kind of privilege was the bishop's authority to govern within the Church. To the Reformers this seemed to be an arbitrary power "to introduce ceremonies in the Church or establish regulations concerning foods, holy days, and the different orders of the clergy" (Art. XXVIII). The Reformers considered such institutions and regulations as, at least in some cases, contrary to the Gospel, and in any case purely optional. Insofar as these "human ordinances" took precedence in the life of the Church, the bishops were held to blame for imposing laws and burdening Christian consciences. When bishops in many dioceses refused to ordain anyone who was involved in the evangelical movement, the Reformers performed ordinations among themselves.

Later Lutheran Interpretations

The decades following 1530 brought not reunion, but a wider and wider rift between the quarreling parties. Lutheranism, as was the case with other groups during the Reformation, was forced to establish a polity quite apart from the authority of the Roman bishop as successor of the apostles. However, none of the confessional works of Lutheranism, written in the sixteenth century, deals with polity. Church order was considered an *adiaphoron*—that is, something not determined by God's word and therefore, at least for the Reformers, not to be required by the Church.

During the early days of the Reformation, Lutherans ordained their own pastors as if there were an emergency situation, without extensive ecclesiastical consideration. Most of the Lutheran interpretations of ordination which are given today derive from theological opinions which were formulated in the nineteenth and twentieth centuries. These interpretations vary considerably. Usually those who offer these interpretations reflect quite as much of their own historical traditions as of their knowledge about the Lutheran confessions. That is, if a Lutheran group was burdened in the old country by a bothersome episcopacy, perhaps associated with an aristocracy that was oppressive of the common people, it arrived in North America extremely opposed to bishops and interpreted the Confessions to support its particular bias. Furthermore, a shortage of Lutheran clergy in the New World meant that non-ordained people were sometimes licensed to act in the place of clergy, thus strengthening an already "high" view of the laity and its role. There is, moreover, much diversity among Lutherans in North America. Until recently Lutheranism was highly ethnic, with the Norwegians, Germans, and several other nationalities keeping to themselves, maintaining their own polity, preserving their own traditions, and having no central hierarchy or governing voice to speak for "Lutheranism" or to resolve disputes.

Some Lutherans view the ministry as being only the universal ministry of all the people of God. Certain persons chosen to lead the group function only for the sake of good order. Sometimes this interpretation suggests that the pastor's Ministry is derived from the ministry of every Christian, but this theory does not appear anywhere in the Lutheran Confessions. The opposite view considers ordained pastors as successors of the apostles and personal representatives of Christ. A third, mediating view sees the sacred Ministry as a divine institution responsible for preaching the Gospel and administering the sacraments, functions for which ordination is essential. These varying interpretations show that in polity Lutheranism can be quite Protestant, quite Catholic, or somewhere in the middle. In North America, the last few decades have brought diverse Lutherans into wide Church unions. Thus, one can find several of these interpretations within a single Church body.

Whichever interpretation is taken, however, several issues tend to receive the same answers. The pastorate is the only indispensable order in Church life. The pastor is needed, for example, to preside at the Eucharist. The pastor acts in the place of Christ, to speak the word, to pronounce absolution and to administer the sacraments. Since these are the sole requirements for the bishop, there is a way in which all Lutheran pastors are bishops in their own place, having the power of bishops and needing no superior to give them sanction.

Breakthroughs in Biblical Studies

As Lutherans and Roman Catholics move toward one another, they are finding that biblical scholarship is supremely helpful for producing consensus. In many issues, biblical scholars find agreement regardless of their denomination or tradition. In the question of apostolic succession such biblical study is proving valuable.

A recent study by the Roman Catholic scholar Raymond E. Brown, for example, has examined priesthood and episcopacy from a New Testament perspective. He finds that the priesthood as the Church now knows it did not exist in New Testament times. We see no direct continuation of the Old Testament levitical priesthood in the early Church. There were several probable reasons for this: Christ was seen as the only priest, or all Christians were viewed as priests, or there was not yet a developed theory of the sacraments that could require an ordained priesthood for sacramental administration. Indeed, some of the most prominent early Christians, such as James who was the leader of the Jerusalem Church, continued until death to participate fully in Jewish worship at the temple. The person who presided at the communal meal which was later called the Eucharist appears to have been one minister among several others, not the unique Minister whom we envision today. Several steps had to be taken before an ordained Christian ministry could develop. First, Christians had to see themselves as members of a religion which was different from Judaism. This movement was still occurring during New Testament times. The destruction of the temple in 70 A.D. also left a void which the Eucharist as sacrifice began to fill.

Instead of priests, the early Church had disciples (the close followers of Jesus), apostles (those sent to serve the Church and the world, the presbyter-bishop (the resident leader of a Christian community), and the president of the Eucharist (who we know in some cases was not the presbyter-bishop). The terms "presbyter" and "bishop" both appear in the New Testament, but there is no suggestion that the bishop was an overseer of several presbyters. By the turn of the first century, however, the situation had stabilized. There was a sacramental ministry in which the presbyter, standing in the apostles' place, was the only one able to preside at the Eucharist, and the bishop had the role of overseeing a group of presbyters as well as serving as a symbol of unity and authority in the Church.

Such biblical studies are extremely important for our continuing discussions today. All too commonly each Christian tradition grounds its practices in specific Bible passages and then condemns other traditions which focus on other Bible passages. We see now that no modern Church order can claim to be *the* early Church order, both because the New Testament is silent on many points and because different communities functioned variously then. Perhaps the most valuable lesson from the New Testament on this question is that differing polities could co-exist within the same communities or between neighboring communities.

Two Irenic Essays

In the Lutheran-Roman Catholic dialogues which have been conducted so far, we find two essays on apostolic succession. The Lutheran essay, after explaining some of the reasons why the Reformers became so antagonistic to the episcopacy, speaks in its favor. The writer shows how both Lutheran and Roman Catholic clergy can be said to stand as the apostles' successors, even though there is no continuation of the apostolic office. However, the Minister stands in the apostolic tradition of preaching the Gospel and administering the sacraments: "Apostolic succession means following in the apostles' footsteps." The sign of this succession, the episcopal laying-on-of-hands, is a good symbol of the unity of the Church which could well be reinstated among Lutherans. Yet "the sign must never be separated from the reality which it signifies, namely the apostolic tradition." The lack of the sign does not mean the loss of the tradition. The move among several American Lutheran groups to call their district or synodical president a "bishop" demonstrates this same awareness concerning the value of the sign of episcopal unity in the Church.

The Roman Catholic essay asks how Rome could recognize a Ministry which exists outside the apostolic succesion Although there is compelling precedent for the Roman Catholic Church not to recognize Protestant ministries as valid, several solutions for dealing with post-Reformation events and declarations can be suggested. Another option is not to deal at all with the past, but to examine the Ministry of Lutheranism today in order to make a contemporary judgment. In addition to the plurality of ministries that co-existed in New Testament times, the Church has had many extraordinary (that is, not ordained in the regular way) ministers of the word and sacraments in the past.

The dialogue goes on. How do we define the bishop? What is the bishop's role? Should there be Church hierarchy? What is the relation of the hierarchy to the local Minister's rights and rites? Who will make what moves? Will the Roman Catholic Church decide that apostolic succession as historically understood is not the only way to validate the Ministry? Will the Lutheran churches alter their understanding of the pastor as bishop and choose episcopal order?

The Ministry of Women

A second issue related to the ordained ministry about which Roman Catholics disagree with Lutherans, as do some Roman Catholics with other Roman Catholics and some Lutherans with other Lutherans, is the ordination of women. In the second century some Christian communities had women as presiders at the Eucharist. Some of those communities were judged heretical, however, because they leaned toward non-Christian Gnostic philosophies, and they were therefore expelled by the orthodox party. It is also true that since the sixteenth-century Reformation, some Protestant denominations have admitted women to ministerial and ecclesial offices on a par with men. However, these denominations have a view of ordination that is quite different from the position of the so-called "sacramental" churches. That is, their ministers are usually elected leaders of the assembly, similar to presidents, and these leaders have no spiritual or sacramental authority beyond that of anyone else. Until quite recently in the "sacramental" churches, namely, Roman Catholicism, Eastern Orthodoxy, Lutheranism and Anglicanism, women priests have seldom been seriously considered.

Now there is a new situation with major divisions of opinion and practice existing in these churches. Although the Orthodox still hardly acknowledge the issue, Episcopalians in the United States ordain women. Some European Lutherans have ordained women in recent decades, although as a rule Lutherans throughout the world do not. In the United States, two major Lutheran bodies now ordain women, one does not, and another leaves the matter to be decided by individual synods. Although Rome is adamant in its objections to women's ordination, various Roman Catholic commissions have been making serious rejoinders to the late Pope Paul VI's statement of opposition in January 1977. One interesting aspect of this debate is that the Lutherans and the Roman Catholics who oppose women's ordination give rather different reasons for their conviction.

Clashing Lutheran Perspectives

The Lutheran Church in America, the American Lutheran Church, and some sections of the Association of Evangelical Lutheran Churches ordain women. While it is impossible outside of a major study to document all the factors that brought about this change, a few can be noted here. Important Lutheran theologians and churchmen in the nineteenth century were unanimously opposed to women pastors. The conservative Lutheran Franz Pieper did not want women even to ask questions in public, and the liberal Samuel Schmucker did not allow women to lead public prayer. Ten years ago, however, the Lutheran Council in the U.S.A. (an association of Lutheran churches) issued studies designed to aid discussion concerning women's ordination. One study, *The Ordination of Women* (ed. Raymond Tiemeyer, 1970), deals particularly with the hermeneutical problem: How do we interpret Scripture? To which portions of Scripture do we give what value? Paul writes that women must keep silence in the assemblies and that they must wear a veil. How do we determine if one, both, or neither of these injunctions is applicable today?

Another influential study supporting the ordination of women, *The Bible and the Role of Women,* was prepared by theologian Krister Stendahl. The essay examines several methods of biblical interpretation and focuses on exegesis of that much-quoted passage in Galatians: "For there is neither Jew nor Greek, there is neither slave nor free, there is no male and female; for you are all one in Christ Jesus." Depending on the method of biblical interpretation, this verse can play a significant role in a person's decision concerning women's ordination. For Stendahl such biblical words prescribe life in the baptized community, a life together in Christ which, since it was not fully realized in New Testament times, is not described in the New Testament narratives or documented by early Church practice. But into that life the Holy Spirit is gradually leading the Church, and for Stendahl that naturally includes both cultural emancipation and the priestly ordination of women.

Despite positive convention action and a decade of women pastors in Lutheranism in the United States, however, there are still many individual Lutherans and even entire Church bodies who oppose women's ordination. Probably the most quoted biblical verse used in condemning women's ordination is St. Paul's injunction: "I permit no woman to teach or have authority over men" (1 Tim. 2:12). Indeed, some conservative Lutheran bodies do not even give congregational voting rights to women.

One influential study opposing the ordination of women has been German Lutheran theologian Peter Brunner's *The Ministry and Ministry of Women* (1959). The central argument in Chapter Four, "Place of Women in Creation," which is often repeated in on-going debates, involves a perceptive, even subtle, exposition of the orders of creation. According to this interpretation of Genesis 1—3, God created the universe to function most properly within divinely instituted orders: the man is the head of the woman; Christ is the head of man; God is the head of Christ (see also 1 Cor. 11:3). Woman is thus subordinate to man—not only the wife to the husband, but every woman to some man. The fall transformed this state of goodness into diabolical oppression, but in Christ the man and the woman are to rediscover the original order of subordination, and through this subordination they become related as Christ is to the Church. It follows for Brunner that since a pastor is the head of the Christian community, the figure of authority, the preacher of the word and the proclaimer of forgiveness, the pastor cannot possibly be a woman.

There is also a small but well-spoken group of Lutherans who oppose women's ordination for a quite different reason. These Lutherans have a passion for eventually reuniting Western Christianity. For them, women's ordination poses still another obstacle for Lutheran-Roman Catholic dialogue.

The Roman Catholic Debate

In January 1977, Pope Paul VI released a statement through the Vatican's Sacred Congregation for the Doctrine of the Faith which opposed women's ordination. The Vatican statement offers reasons for its objections which are quite different from the usual Lutheran argument about the subordination of women. In fact the accompanying commentary "discarded a fair number of explanations given by medieval theologians . . . (who) claimed to find their basis in an inferiority of women vis-à-vis man. . . . " Nor does the Vatican statement focus on individual Bible passages. Instead it appeals more to tradition and to symbolic levels of understanding. The statement first recalls the Church's tradition of opposition to women's ordination. For a Church in which the witness of the past is heard so respectfully, this appeal to tradition is no small point. Second, it is argued, Jesus did not extend his apostolic charge to any women. Third, even though there was a revolutionary "high" view of women within the early Church, the apostles maintained Jesus' practice nonetheless, and women were not the official proclaimers of the Gospel. This attitude of Jesus and his apostles remains of permanent value, indeed of normative character for the Church.

The second half of the Vatican statement is dedicated to a careful discussion of "the ministerial priesthood in light of the mystery of Christ." The priest stands *in persona Christi,* that is, in the place of Christ. The sacramental nature of the priesthood lies in the fact that it is a sign of the mystery of Christ, and this mystery is explored in numerous biblical images which describe Christ as male and his people, the Church, as female. To depict the priesthood authentically, the person "in the place of Christ" must therefore be male. The mystery of the Church forbids applying secular logic to allow women's ordination. Although the Vatican statement affirmed the equality of baptized persons, it did not translate that equality into a permission to ordain women within this mystery of Christ.

Some objections to the Vatican statement have come from biblical scholars who say that it is misleading to argue that just because Jesus called only men, only men can be priests. Biblical scholars tend to agree that the twelve disciples were a singular phenomenon and that the characteristics of such a unique calling do not apply to the present question of women's ordination. Secondly, the New Testament Church did not espouse one polity which can be said to descend directly from Jesus and thus inform modern practice. That Church had no priests as we know them.

An influential work by Haye Van der Meer, S.J., *Women Priests in the Catholic Church? A Theological-Historical Investigation,* examines the judgments of various Church Fathers who opposed leadership by women in order to determine the presuppositions which lay behind their opposition. Van der Meer finds that those presuppositions are almost universally rejected today. If a Church Father excluded women from leadership because he judged them "without much intelligence," can we reject his reasons and still retain his conclusions today? The issue of the symbolic representation of Christ by the male priest is also being addressed. R. A. Norris in "The Ordination of Women and the 'Maleness' of Christ" states that in the christological discussions which occurred during the Church's early centuries, the incarnation was described as God becoming a human being in Jesus Christ, rather than God becoming a male in Jesus. The significance of Jesus as Christ lies not in his maleness but in his being the Christ. Baptism grants to all Christians, to women as well as to men, an incorporation into Christ. The author claims that an ordained female can represent the Christ of the baptismal mystery as much as any male can.

A Basic Link

Questions concerning the meaning of ordination take on varied emphases. Is the ordained Ministry a function dependent only on the ability to perform it? Or is it an office dependent also on the Church's appointment? Another way to address the issue appears like a grammar lesson. *Can* the Church ordain women? *May* the Church ordain women? *Should* the Church ordain women? The issue of women's ordination is especially interesting for the Lutheran-Roman Catholic dialogue. While the battles rage within each Church body, agreements are being discovered across denominational lines in that dialogue. While the kinds of arguments we raise are often the products of our traditions—that is, do we argue from Scripture or from tradition?—our denominational labels are not always an indication of our positions on controverted issues. We have links to one another in the body of Christ through our baptism which surmount the obstacles placed before us in celebrating the Eucharist and in understanding the Ministry.

FOR STUDY AND DISCUSSION

1. The creed uses four adjectives to describe the Church—one, holy, catholic, apostolic. What does each of these terms mean to Roman Catholics and to Lutherans?
2. What is the most basic meaning of the word "Church"?
3. What is the derivation of each of the following words: deacon, priest, pastor, presbyter, bishop? How do Lutherans and Roman Catholics differ in their ordinary usage of each of these terms?
4. What is the process through which one enters the "specialized Ministry" in each of our communions?
5. What is the apostolic succession in the Roman Catholic view? How do Lutherans view this term?
6. What are three views of the Ministry found among contemporary Lutherans?
7. How do priests or other Ministers of the Church relate to the Old Testament priesthood? To the various offices named in the New Testament?
8. How do Lutherans and Roman Catholics differ in their understanding of the necessity of a particular Church order? At what points are they agreed on matters of church order?
9. What are the pros and cons of the ordination of women as currently debated among Lutherans? Among Roman Catholics?

FOR FURTHER READING

William E. Diehl, *Christianity and Real Life* (Philadelphia: Fortress Press).

Peter Brunner, *The Ministry and the Ministry of Women* (St. Louis: Concordia Publishing House).

Krister Stendahl, *The Bible and the Role of Women* (Philadelphia: Fortress Press).

Milo Brekke *et al, Ten Faces of Ministry* (Minneapolis: Augsburg
    Publishing House).

Raymond Brown, *Priest and Bishop* (New York: Paulist Press).

Paul C. Empie and T. Austin Murphy, eds., *Lutherans and Catholics
    in Dialogue IV—Eucharist and Ministry* (Minneapolis: Augs-
    burg Publishing House).

5. Authority: The Petrine Ministry

"I for my part declare to you, you are 'Rock,' and on this rock I will build my Church, and the jaws of death shall not prevail against it. I will entrust to you the keys of the kingdom of heaven. Whatever you declare bound on earth shall be bound in heaven; whatever you declare loosed on earth shall be loosed in heaven" (Mt. 16:18–19). Many issues continue to divide Lutherans and Roman Catholics, but one of the most serious—and certainly the most emotionally charged—is the papacy, the role of the Pope, the bishop of Rome. Pope Paul VI rightly noted this in 1967: "The Pope—as we all know—is undoubtedly the gravest obstacle in the path of ecumenism." That obstacle remains today as it has for centuries.

The papacy is part of Roman Catholic identity. It is also a feature of Roman Catholicism which often troubles Lutherans the most. Each group has defended its own position over the centuries and, until recently, there seemed little hope of a reasonable discussion on this touchy subject. At root, the question is one of Church authority and its relationship to the Scriptures. Is the papacy a *necessary* or simply a *useful* instrument of order and unity in the universal Church? Is the papacy an expression of God's will for the Church or merely a human institution designed to promote unity? In this chapter, we will consider these and other questions concerning papal authority. Because historical and cultural events played such an important part in the development of the two Churches, this chapter is divided into three parts, dealing with the past, the present, and the future. Let us begin with the troublesome times of the sixteenth century.

I
THE PAST

The year 1530 was a tumultuous one. On the one hand, Martin Luther, who had already made clear his opposition to Rome on several occasions and who had finally been excommunicated in 1521, continued to attract thousands of followers, including many powerful princes. The unity of Western Christianity was clearly deteriorating, and there seemed no hope of healing the breach. On the other hand, the Holy Roman Empire faced a serious military threat from the Turks. In 1530, having already occupied most of Hungary, 350,000 Turkish troops laid siege to Vienna.

Emperor Charles V, only thirty years old at the time, convoked the Diet of Augsburg in an attempt to heal the religious differences in the empire and to unite the people against "the infidel enemy." He asked the Lutherans to prepare a statement of their beliefs. For them, it was an opportunity to defend themselves against many current misunderstandings of their position and to provide a summary of their theological views that would be acceptable both to the emperor and to Rome. The intention of the Lutherans was to demonstrate their orthodoxy and to show the emperor that they were not heretics but loyal to the faith of the Catholic Church.

Confessional Intention

On June 25, 1530, the now famous Augsburg Confession was read aloud in German before the emperor in the bishop's palace—so clearly that the people in the courtyard could hear it. The Confession was moderate, positive, and conciliatory. Signed by seven imperial princes and two representatives from the free cities of the empire, the Confession displayed a willingness to compromise on the Lutheran side. Its principal author was Philip Melanchthon, a brilliant thirty-three-year-old layman committed to Church reform.

The signers of the Confession were not interested in beginning a schism. Rather, they wished to emphasize their continuity with the ancient Church. Thus, Article XXI stated: "As can be seen, there is nothing here that departs from the Scriptures or the Catholic Church or the Church of Rome, insofar as the ancient Church is known to us from its writers." The Augsburg Confession is not a complicated theological document. It is a public statement of faith. It is recognized by Lutherans as a basic confession, a standard for interpreting Scripture and for apostolic preaching and writing. The Confession is an important historical document as well, and it has been likened to the Magna Carta, the Declaration of Independence, and the United Nations' Declaration of the Rights of Man.

At first, some Lutherans felt that the Confession was too indecisive. They wanted a stronger declaration of Lutheran beliefs and accused Melanchthon of being a "pussyfooter." Catholic leaders felt that the Confession amounted to "throwing dust in the eyes of the emperor," since it failed to mention the critical issues of the papacy, purgatory, and indulgences. In the end, the two parties were unable to agree. Not until four centuries later would a genuine hope for reunion be rekindled.

Papacy and Scripture

What does the Augsburg Confession tell us about papal authority? Although there is no direct reference to this subject, there are several indications in the Confession and in other writings that reveal the Lutheran position. Lutherans have always placed greater emphasis on pure doctrine than on Church organization. For them, the ultimate norm of all authority in the Church, including papal authority, is Jesus Christ revealed in the Gospel. The Scriptures are considered as a testimony to the power that saves sinful humanity, not simply some words on a printed page. For example, the Formula of Concord (1577) affirmed that the only norm of faith is the prophetic and apostolic writings of the Old and New Testaments. Martin Luther's dramatic assertion at the Diet of Worms revealed that same view:

> Unless I am convicted by Scripture and plain reason—I do not accept the authority of Popes and councils, for they have contradicted each other—my conscience is captive to the word of God. I cannot and I will not recant anything, for to go against my conscience is neither right nor safe. God help me. Amen.

Roman Catholics, of course, did not deny that God is the source of all authority. Although they believed in a Church tightly organized around the Pope, bishops, and priests, they could say with St.

Paul: "There is no authority except from God" (Rom. 13:1). Catholics also accepted the privileged role of the Scriptures—that special way by which God has disclosed himself to the world. Nothing can be proposed as an article of faith that is not rooted in some way in the Scriptures. Catholics, however, believed that the Church, under the guidance of the Holy Spirit, could teach authoritatively in general councils and in certain pronouncements of the Pope and bishops. In the Roman Catholic view, post-biblical tradition should be accepted with as much respect as the Scriptures are received.

In the angry atmosphere of the sixteenth century, Lutherans charged Roman Catholics with rejecting the Scriptures as a norm of faith, and Catholics accused Lutherans of denying the value of the councils or later Church pronouncements. Both sides exaggerated and misrepresented the position of their adversaries. As the ecumenical dialogues of the twentieth century have shown, the two Churches have much more in common than at first appears. One of the tragedies of the sixteenth century was that the heated debate did not move into more constructive dialogue.

If the Lutherans argued for the superiority of the Scriptures as the ultimate norm for all ecclesiastical organization, discipline, and doctrine, the Church in their view was not a vague, purely spiritual reality. They did not do away with authority. The Augsburg Confession described the Church as "the assembly of all believers, among whom the Gospel is preached in all its purity and the holy sacraments are administered according to the Gospal" (Art. III). Furthermore, authority is necessary in the Church for the sake of good order and peace: "Nobody should publicly teach or preach or administer the sacraments without a regular call" (Art. IV). The Confession also declared that bishops have the responsibility to preach the Gospel, forgive sins, judge correct doctrine and, if the occasion arises, condemn any doctrine that is contrary to the Gospel (Art. XXVIII).

The fundamental theme of the Lutheran reformers, which is reflected in the Augsburg Confession, is the opposition to all forms of mediation between God and humanity which keep human beings in a state of subjection and dependence. A favorite Lutheran text was: "There is only one mediator between God and mankind, himself a man, Christ Jesus, who sacrificed himself as a ransom for all" (1 Tim. 2:5–6). Thus, the Lutherans rejected the emphasis which Catholics placed on good works, the intercession of the saints, and, as the Confession mentions, priestly celibacy and monastic vows. They also had difficulty with Roman Catholic teachings on the papacy.

It should be noted here that the early Lutherans were not opposed to Catholicism as such, or even to the papacy in itself. In fact, they considered themselves Catholics and took it for granted that the papacy, if reformed, was capable of providing a universal ministry among Christians. The early Lutherans, nevertheless, were opposed to individual Popes and spoke out against the abuses that had grown up around the office. They called for an ecumenical council to reform the papacy according to the Gospel.

Smalcald Articles

What began as a desire to reform the papacy ended in a rejection of the papacy. Seven years after Roman Catholic representatives judged the Augsburg Confession unacceptable, the Smalcald Articles appeared. Written by Martin Luther, they lacked the moderate tone of the Confession and dealt directly with the papacy. The papacy was criticized for tyranny, deception, blasphemy, and unsurpation of authority. Luther denied that the pope was head of the Church "by divine right," although he was willing to admit that the Pope was the legitimate head of the diocese of Rome and could exercise authority "by human right" over those churches which freely placed themselves under his care. Luther took a strong line against the papacy: "The papacy is of no use to the Church because it exercises no Christian office" (Section II, Article IV). He continued: "The Pope is the real Antichrist who has raised himself over and set himself against Christ, for the Pope will not permit Christians to be saved except by his own power which amounts to nothing, since it is neither established nor commanded by God."

By 1537, therefore, Lutherans generally had rejected the papacy and denied that it was willed by God. The papacy was considered simply a human institution, and papal claims to divine origin were regarded as unsupported by the Scriptures. Both Luther and Melanchthon agreed that since the Pope was a tyrannical ruler, the Antichrist, Christians should not be subject to his authority. Although Luther saw no hope for a possible reform of the papacy, Melanchthon was more optimistic. As one of the signers of the Smalcald Articles, he added the following note alongside his signature: "However, concerning the Pope, I hold that, if he would allow the Gospel, we too may concede to him that superiority over the bishops which he possesses by human right, making this concession for the sake of peace and general unity among the Christians who are now under him and may be in the future."

Rome's Reaction

Rome viewed the Lutheran position as an attack on the integrity and unity of the Church. Lutherans were, according to Rome, outside the true Church. Rome was especially sensitive to the Lutheran attack on papal authority as demonstrated in the Augsburg Confession's repudiation of priestly celibacy and monastic vows, both of which had long-standing papal support. Moreover, Roman Catholics believed that the office of the papacy was instituted by Jesus Christ when he established Peter as head of the Church. The papacy, then, is "of divine right," and as such cannot be set aside. Rome also took issue with the theory of mediation proposed by the Lutherans. While there is only one mediator of redemption, Jesus Christ, there are many mediators of intercession, such as the saints. Likewise, just as the Scriptures and the ancient creeds mediate God's revelation to his people, so too the papacy is a mediating agent which serves to protect and explain the true meaning of the Christ-event in time.

The Church of Rome gradually began to realize that many of the abuses criticized by the Lutherans would have to be corrected. In the sixteenth century, the Church had fallen victim to a spirit of worldliness. The clergy were often poorly trained; the preaching of the word and administration of the sacraments were being improperly performed; the papal and episcopal courts were frequently places of greed and luxury. To remedy this deplorable situation, the Pope convoked the Council of Trent (1545–1563) which devoted itself to doctrinal and disciplinary reform. The council began a new era for the Roman Catholic Church. The Lutherans did not attend the Council of Trent, and, despite some negotiations between the two Churches during the next two hundred years, efforts at reunion were unsuccessful.

II
THE PRESENT

Today, the relationship between Lutherans and Roman Catholics has improved immensely. Dialogue has replaced debate, and hostility has given way to hope. One of the principal reasons for this attitudinal change was the convocation of the Second Vatican Council (1962–1965) by Pope John XXIII. Many thought that he would be simply a "caretaker Pope," because he was elected when he was seventy-six. Providence had other plans for him. A warm, outgoing person, Pope John was loved immediately by believers and unbelievers alike. There is no doubt that the signers of the Augsburg Confession would have found him sympathetic and caring and would have applauded his idea of calling a council. "Good Pope John," as he is often called, intended that the Second Vatican Council should be a council of reform and reunion. He felt that the Roman Catholic Church had to renew itself if it was to work effectively for Christian unity.

In the *Decree on Ecumenism,* the Second Vatican Council lamented the fact that Christians are divided and noted that "men of both sides were to blame" (Art. 3). It further noted that all Christians must resort to Jesus Christ as the center and source of Church unity. The council also listed those elements in the life of the Church of Jesus Christ which are present outside the visible boundaries of the Roman Catholic Church: the sacraments, especially baptism and the Eucharist; the written word of God; the life of grace; the virtues of faith, hope, and charity; the gifts of the Holy Spirit. In addition, the council pointed out that all Christians share in a common mission to proclaim Jesus Christ to the world, to render worship and obedience to God the Father, and to spread the Gospel of justice and peace. Lutherans, along with other Christian Churches and communities, participated as observers at the Second Vatican Council. They attended all its sessions, received the drafts of conciliar documents, and were invited to communicate their reactions through the Secretariat for Promoting Christian Unity. The experience of the council was valuable for both Lutherans and Roman Catholics; it enabled both Churches to realize the urgency of working together for unity.

The United States Dialogue

One of the most productive ecumenical efforts since the council came to a close has been the Lutheran-Roman Catholic dialogue in the United States. Since 1965, representatives of the two traditions have been engaged in a series of theological conversations and have been able to reach remarkable consensus on many controversial issues. The question of Church authority was the subject of the fifth dialogue. After that dialogue was completed, two studies were published: *Peter in the New Testament* (1973) and *Papal Primacy and the Universal Church* (1974). The sixth dialogue produced a common statement on "Teaching Authority and Infallibility in the Church" (1978). These exciting documents are the result of years of careful study and discussion. They are honest, hopeful, and charitable. Their aim is clear: "Neither Church should continue to tolerate a situation in which members of one communion look upon the other as alien" (Dialogue V, #34, p. 23).

The Second Vatican Council and the Lutheran-Roman Catholic dialogues in the United States are our best sources for understanding the present status of relations between Roman Catholics and Lutherans. On the question of the papacy, there are, of course, agreements and disagreements. Here we will first discuss what unites Lutherans and Roman Catholics. Then we will consider the major problems that still divide us.

Five Points of Agreement

First, a consensus exists that in addition to the spiritual unity of the Church, a visible, concrete manifestation of that unity should be expressed in a particular ministry of the Church. The fifth Lutheran-Roman Catholic dialogue in the United States, for example, stated that Lutherans have a growing awareness "of the necessity of a specific ministry to serve the Church's unity and universal mission" (#4, p. 10). That ministry would demonstrate clearly that the Church is the *one* body of Christ, a single people of God, a sign of the unity of all people in Jesus Christ at the end-time. An ordering, unifying ministry would help local churches throughout the world to relate to the universal Church. Such a ministry, therefore, would provide the world with a credible, visible witness to Christian unity. The fifth dialogue called such a ministry the "Petrine function." It is described as "a particular form of ministry exercised by a person, officeholder, or local church with reference to the Church as a whole" (#4, p. 11). The purpose of such a ministry would be "to promote or preserve the oneness of the Church by symbolizing unity, and by facilitating communication, mutual assistance, or correction, and collaboration in the Church's mission" (#4, p. 12).

Second, the two churches have agreed that the ministry which is to be responsible for the universal Church may be held by one individual or, at least, that such a possibility "cannot be ruled out on the basis of the biblical evidence" (#29, p. 22). The participants examined the New Testament and concluded that Peter played a special role in the apostolic community. He is listed first among the twelve; he was one of the first to be called; he was the first apostolic witness to the risen Lord; he was frequently the spokesman and leader of the apostles; he was active in missionary work. Among all the companions of Jesus, Peter was the most prominent. His activities suggest that he was involved in a broad ministry to the other churches after the resurrection of Jesus.

In the New Testament, there are many images associated with Peter: "missionary, fisherman, pastoral shepherd, martyr, recipient of special revelation, confessor of the true faith, magisterial protector, and repentant sinner" (*Peter in the New Testament*, p. 166). These biblical images developed more fully later on: "The ecumenical discussion must involve not only the historical figure [of Peter] but also the continuing trajectory" (*Peter in the New Testament*, p. 168). After the first century, the Church developed some of these images of Peter in a way that was not inconsistent with the Scriptures. The Lutheran-Roman Catholic dialogue has insisted that the centralization of the Petrine function in one person (the Pope) was the result of a long process of development. It also noted that the subsequent development of the papacy was not opposed to the Scriptures and not contrary to the role which Peter held in the apostolic Church.

Third, the participants in the dialogue have agreed that the Pope has in many ways exercised a truly beneficial ministry for the churches under his care. In fact, the fifth dialogue noted that the bishop of Rome has been "the single most notable representative" of the Petrine ministry to the universal Church. Furthermore, the Lutheran participants have also recognized the value of the historic papacy. They said that the papacy unified the Christian West when it was threatened by non-Christian forces, defended the independence of the Church from control by the state, and effectively promoted social justice.

Fourth, Lutherans and Roman Catholics in the dialogue have reached some consensus on the doctrine of infallibility—that "charism of truth" by which the Church is protected from error when teaching about matters of faith and morals. The principal conclusion of the sixth dialogue was that "the ultimate trust of Christians is in Christ and the Gospel, not in a doctrine of infallibility, whether of Scripture, the Church, or the Pope" ("Common Statement," #51). Both Lutherans and Roman Catholics believe in the "indefectibility" of the Church and are convinced that God will remain with his people and keep his Church faithful to the Gospel until the end of time. Likewise, the participants in the dialogue agreed that it is fitting there should be a universal teaching authority in the Church with the twofold task of assuring the correct proclamation of the Gospel and of reformulating doctrine in accord with the Scriptures. The sixth dialogue placed infallibility "in the theological categories of promise, trust, and hope, rather than in the juridical categories of law, obligation, and obedience" ("Roman Catholic Reflections," #5).

Fifth, Lutherans and Roman Catholics in the dialogue agreed that the papacy needs continual reform. As we saw earlier, this was also the desire of those who composed the Augsburg Confession. The papacy must be adaptable and must discover new ways of functioning if it is to meet the needs of the contemporary Church. The style of papal authority does not have to be tied irrevocably to unchanging patterns of the past. Such reform will help make the papacy less imperialistic, less remote, and less legalistic at the same time as it becomes more pastoral, more involved, and more sensitive. The criterion for reform must be the Gospel. Thus, the Lutheran participants in the fifth dialogue said that "any form of papal primacy that does not fully safeguard the freedom of the Gospel is unacceptable to Lutherans" (#38, p. 32). The Roman Catholic participants affirmed that "the papacy must be understood in ways that recognize the Church's total subordination to Christ and the Gospel" (p. 36).

Principles of Reform

The fifth dialogue gave three principles which should be applied when reforming the papacy: legitimate diversity, collegiality, and subsidiarity. The first of these, legitimate diversity, means that unity, not uniformity, is the goal. There is room in the Church for various forms of piety, liturgy, custom, and law. The Augsburg Confession made a similar assertion: "It is not necessary for the true unity of the Christian church that ceremonies, instituted by men, should be observed uniformly in all places" (Art. VII).

The second principle of reform, collegiality, means cooperation or shared responsibility. The Second Vatican Council emphasized this principle in order to encourage the initiative and assistance of all the members of the Church. The synod of bishops, the national episcopal conferences, priests' senates, and parish councils are all organs of collegiality or shared decision-making. Collegiality is the opposite of centralization and is designed to foster collaboration. Because the problems facing the modern Church are so complex, it is impossible for one person to deal with all of them. The Pope must work closely with the bishops in reaching decisions which affect the entire Church; bishops, priests, and laity must likewise collaborate in the life of the local church.

The third principle of reform, subsidiarity, refers to the responsibility and freedom that should be given to local churches and communities for making their own decisions. The ideal is this: Local communities should make decisions locally whenever possible and without recourse to higher authority. Unity among the churches must, of course, be preserved, but it is not necessary that in every instance centralized authority should make decisions for the local churches.

These three norms for renewal of the papacy reflect the Christian belief that the Holy Spirit operates in all parts of the Church, not just among Church leaders. If these norms continue to be applied to the papacy, many Lutheran objections will be answered after some time has passed. The hopes implied in the Augsburg Confession for a reformed papacy would thus eventually be fulfilled. The Lutheran participants in the fifth dialogue have said: "We cannot responsibly dismiss the possibility that some form of the papacy, renewed and restructured under the Gospel, may be an appropriate expression of the ministry that serves the unity and ordering of the Church" (#32, p. 28). Such a reform would make the Pope less of a monarch and more of a pastoral leader. It would introduce a series of checks and balances through collegial government, and it would situate the papacy more clearly in the context of the entire Church.

These five areas of agreement between Lutherans and Roman Catholics in dialogue are significant and substantial. They do not solve all the problems, but they are important steps on the road to reunion. They were achieved because each group was faithful to its own heritage and was also open to the guidance of the Holy Spirit. However, there still are some issues that must be resolved. In the next section, we will consider some of those disagreements. The three major obstacles are found in the Roman Catholic teachings about the divine institution of the papacy, the primacy of jurisdiction, and the infallibility of the pope.

Three Major Obstacles

The first obstacle concerns the divine institution of the papacy. Has the papacy been instituted by God through Jesus, or is it only an institution of human origin? Roman Catholics have traditionally linked Peter with the papacy, and they believe that there is a scriptural basis for at least some of the papal claims. For Catholics, then, the papacy is willed by God. It is "of divine right," an instrument of God by which the unity of the Church is maintained. Roman Catholics hold that the papacy is an historic office which continues the functions exercised by Peter and the other apostles.

Lutherans, on the other hand, have always held that the papacy is a human institution. It may be useful, beneficial, even desirable at times, but it is still only "of human right." This point was made in the fourth dialogue which noted that the Lutheran confessional writings "do not exclude the possibility that the papacy may have a symbolical or functional value in a wider area as long as its primacy is seen as being of human right" (#29, p. 20). For Lutherans, the papacy is not the only way the Petrine function can be present in the Church: "There is . . . no single or uniquely legitimate form of the exercise of the Petrine function" (Dialogue V, #34, p. 30). Compare this statement with the Roman Catholic assertion that the papal office, although it must always be reformed, is essential to the Church:

"We cannot foresee any set of circumstances that would make it desirable, even if it were possible, to abolish the papal office" (Dialogue V, p. 37). The question returns, then, to the divine quality of the papal office and its enduring place in the Church.

A difficult problem for both Lutherans and Roman Catholics is the relationship between Peter and the bishops of Rome. The fifth dialogue noted that "from the New Testament we know nothing of a succession to Peter in Rome" (#11, p. 14). Historians in both traditions generally agree that the early Popes did not clearly function as universal authorities in the Church until the third or fourth centuries. Because of this time-gap, Lutherans are skeptical about the divine institution of the papacy and thus argue that it is a human institution. Catholics, however, believe that the development of the papacy is rooted in Peter's role among the apostles and that this development was accomplished under the direction of the Holy Spirit present in the Church. In that sense, therefore, the papacy can be called "divinely willed." Obviously, much more study and dialogue is required before this disputed point can be resolved.

Jurisdiction

A second obstacle is the meaning of papal authority or jurisdiction. According to the Second Vatican Council, which in fact repeated the teaching of the First Vatican Council, the "Roman Pontiff has full, supreme, and universal power over the Church, and he can always exercise this power freely" (*Constitution on the Church,* Art. 22). The Pope, then, is the human head of the Church and nobody, even an ecumenical council, can override his decision as long as he is the legitimate Pope. The Second Vatican Council also declared the doctrine of collegiality and stated that "together with its head, the Roman Pontiff, and never without this head, the episcopal order [college] is the subject of supreme and full power over the universal Church" (*Constitution on the Church,* Art. 22). One of the major tasks of the present papacy is to implement this doctrine of collegiality according to which the pope and the bishops would act together in making decisions affecting the universal Church. Collegial government and shared responsibility should characterize the future papacy. Papal primacy should be conceived as a gift of the Holy Spirit and as a service to the entire community of believers. If papal structures were renewed according to this ideal, it would be less objectionable to Lutherans.

The fifth Roman Catholic-Lutheran dialogue in the United States did not spell out in detail how papal reform should proceed. It spoke about a pastoral and symbolic papacy, but it did not discuss its jurisdictional elements. We saw earlier that Melanchthon saw the possibility, "for the sake of peace and general unity," that the Pope might exercise "authority over the bishops." The fifth dialogue did not go that far, although it did not reject such a possibility. For centuries, Lutherans have considered papal authority as synonymous with "arbitrary authoritarianism." Although the fifth dialogue stated that "one may foresee that voluntary limitations by the Pope of the exercise of his jurisdiction will accompany the growing vitality of the organs of collegial government" (#24, p. 21), many Lutherans feel little progress has been made. Since we are now at the beginning of a new pontificate, there is added hope that Pope John Paul II will continue to reform the papal office in ways that will enable the Pope once again to be "the pastor and teacher of all Christians."

Infallibility

The third obstacle is the doctrine of infallibility. The term "infallibility" is not found in the Lutheran tradition, and, in fact, infallibility was defined as a Roman Catholic dogma only in 1870 at the First Vatican Council. The main objection of the Lutherans is that the doctrine of infallibility undercuts the unique role of Jesus Christ and the normative function of the Scriptures by seemingly placing the Pope above them. However, the Second Vatican Council helped clarify the matter when it stated that the teaching office of the Church "is not above the word of God, but serves it, teaching only what has been handed on, listening to it devoutly, guarding it scrupulously, and explaining it faithfully by divine commission" (*Constitution on Divine Revelation,* Art. 10).

The sixth Lutheran-Roman Catholic dialogue on "Teaching Authority and Infallibility in the Church" has done much to dispel many mutual misunderstandings. The Lutherans were able to agree that Roman Catholics do not hold a doctrine that was opposed to the Gospel, and Catholics began to realize that Lutheran reluctance to speak about infallibility is in no way an indication of any lack of trust that the Lord will assist the Church in faithfully proclaiming the Gospel. Both sides agreed that the Church is "indefectible," that it does not ultimately go astray, and that some kind of teaching authority is necessary in the Church. Despite the fact that a Pope has proclaimed only one infallible teaching since 1870—Pius XII's definition of Mary's assumption in 1950—many Lutherans are nonetheless uneasy about the claim that the Pope can speak without error in matters of faith and morals when certain conditions are fulfilled. The three obstacles that still divide Lutherans and Roman Catholics have deep historical roots and continue to challenge both traditions. Although significant progress has been made in resolving these difficult issues, continued study, reflection, and prayer will be necessary.

III
THE FUTURE

The last fifteen years have contributed more to the relationship between Lutherans and Roman Catholics than the previous four centuries. It is impossible to chart the course which the ecumenical movement will take in the years ahead. Today we hear frequently that interest in Christian unity has waned and that Christians have lost much of the enthusiasm which they had in the late 1960's. Furthermore, the hopes of the participants in the Lutheran-Roman Catholic dialogues are not completely shared by all the members of their respective Churches. There is still an anti-ecumenical spirit among many Lutherans and Roman Catholics who feel that the dialogues are nothing but a "sell-out," a watering-down of a unique heritage. Some Catholics believe that there is no ecumenical problem at all; if Lutherans want to return to the Church, then let them become Roman Catholics. There are also Lutherans who think that Lutheranism has survived for nearly five hundred years without a Pope and can continue to do so. That attitude is somewhat due to the length of time the two Churches have been divided. A certain amount of indifference and perhaps even hostility to the "other" seems to be ingrained in Church members on both sides. Their negative attitude is also due partly to a fear of change and possible compromise. The "one true Church of the future" still remains an unknown quantity that causes many to be apprehensive.

To overcome this reluctance concerning ecumenism, we all will have to confront our own prejudices and partisan loyalties. We have to ask ourselves the question: Is not the present division among Christians quite contrary to the will of Jesus Christ that the Church should be one? If our answer is affirmative, then we have to make every effort to overcome the narrowness of our religious views, to rid ourselves of petty sectarianism, and to commit ourselves with God's grace and love to work for the union of all Christians.

The following suggestions concerning the future direction of ecumenical efforts among Lutherans and Roman Catholics are offered in the spirit of the Augsburg Confession and the Second Vatican Council, both of which were instruments of reform and reunion. They are made in the hope that in the future the papacy will not be a barrier to reconciliation.

First, the dialogue between Lutherans and Roman Catholics must continue. Not only should the official theological conversations between representatives of the two Churches proceed as planned, but the results of past accords should be shared with the rest of the believing community. It is most important that lay people become aware of the progress that has been made. The reality of ecumenism has to be communicated to the parishes. Parishes should form groups to read and discuss the dialogues as well as the main confessional writings of both traditions. There should be joint Bible study, shared prayer, and cooperation in mission and pastoral care. Both churches should carefully examine their catechetical and teaching materials so that any historical or doctrinal distortions are corrected.

Second, serious thought should also be given to establishing some kind of canonical status that would include Lutherans and Roman Catholics in a form of institutional unity. This move toward formal affiliation might begin with altar and pulpit fellowship as well as a mutual recognition of ministries and sacraments in light of the agreements that have already been reached. This development could occur before complete agreement on all doctrinal issues is reached. In such an institutional association, Lutherans would recognize the Pope's role of leadership, but they would have a different relationship to him than Roman Catholics. The Lutheran churches would preserve their own traditions and would be self-governing. They would be considered sister churches which, despite their differences, would truly be part of a wider Church unity. The details of such an association would have to be delineated carefully in advance in order to avoid anything that might smack of inequality or paternalism.

The proposal to establish a canonical affiliation between Lutherans and Roman Catholics is not new. It should be remembered that the Augsburg Confession expressed the Lutherans' desire to remain Catholic and still retain their particular interpretations of the Christian faith. Over the centuries and quite recently, Lutheran theologians have insisted that Lutheranism is not a separate Church but is rather a movement within and for the one, holy, catholic, apostolic Church. A canonical association with the Roman Catholic Church might be an appropriate development of such a position.

Third, it should be asked if, in the future, an ecumenical or general council should be convoked in which all Christians would participate. The Augsburg Confession called for a "general, free, and Christian council" to settle existing differences. The Roman Catholic Church did not accept that suggestion. Later, when the Council of Trent was convoked in 1545, the Lutherans did not attend. At the present time, such a proposal for a general council might seem premature, but it should not be completely ruled out for the future. Before the council could become a reality, however, the two Churches would have to become far more closely associated than they are today. There would have to be further agreement on disputed questions, a series of meetings between the Pope and Lutheran leaders, greater exchange, and sacramental sharing. In the event that a pan-Christian ecumenical council should be deemed feasible, it would have to be carefully planned by the convoking Churches. There would have to be agreement beforehand on agenda, membership, leadership, voting rights, and the type of authority which the council would be considered to possess. Each of these items raises immense theological and practical questions.

Fourth, any advance toward the reunion of Lutherans and Roman Catholics cannot be accomplished without recourse to prayer. The Second Vatican Council wisely observed that "there can be no ecumenism worthy of the name without interior conversion" (*Decree on Ecumenism,* Art. 7). Ecumenism is a gift that should be the object of our prayer. Hard work, brilliant theological reflection, and persuasive preaching are all important, but of themselves they will not produce unity. The unity of all in Jesus Christ will ultimately be a gift from God. The closer that Christians unite with the Father, the Son, and the Spirit, the easier it will be for them to unite with one another. As we observe the 450th anniversary of the Augsburg Confession, it is an appropriate time to rededicate ourselves to Christian unity and to say with St. Paul: "I can do all things in him who strengthens me" (Phil.4:13.)

FOR STUDY AND DISCUSSION

1. What is the basic question that divides Roman Catholics and Lutherans regarding the papacy? What are several ways in which that basic question can be expressed?
2. What was the historical context in which the Augsburg Confession was written?
3. What do the Lutheran confessional writings say about the papacy?
4. What were the central points of dispute between Lutherans and Roman Catholics concerning the papacy in the sixteenth century?
5. What were the *Smalcald Articles* and what was their significance?
6. How did the Church of Rome react to the sixteenth-century Lutheran positions on the papacy?
7. How has the relationship between Lutherans and Roman Catholics changed today and what are the reasons for the change?
8. What are the several points of agreement on the papacy which contemporary Lutherans and Roman Catholics share? How is each point of agreement explained in detail?
9. What are the principles for reform and renewal of the papacy which have been developed by the Lutheran-Roman Catholic dialogue in the United States? What effect would the application of these principles have on Lutheran-Roman Catholic relations today?
10. Describe the three major obstacles regarding the papacy which still divide Lutherans and Roman Catholics.
11. What is meant by the phrase "of divine right"? Why is the teaching an obstacle to agreement?

12. What is the scope and extent of the Pope's jurisdiction according to Roman Catholics? How do Lutherans view the matter?
13. What is meant by papal "infallibility"? How is papal "infallibility" different from the "indefectibility" of the Church?
14. Will full agreement on the Petrine ministry ever be reached by Lutherans and Roman Catholics?
15. Discuss the value and significance of the suggestions made in this chapter for improving relations between Lutherans and Roman Catholics.

FOR FURTHER READING

"The Graymoor Papers: Papacy in Ecumenical Perspective," *Journal of Ecumenical Studies,* XIII, 3 (Summer 1976), pp. 345–404.

Paul C. Empie and T. Austin Murphy, eds., *Lutherans and Catholics in Dialogue V—Papal Primacy and the Universal Church* (Minneapolis: Augsburg Publishing House).

Joseph Burgess, ed., *Lutherans and Catholics in Dialogue VI— Teaching Authority and Infallibility in the Church* (Minneapolis: Augsburg Publishing House).

Raymond E. Brown, Karl P. Donfriend, and John Reumann, eds., *Peter in the New Testament* (Minneapolis: Augsburg Publishing House, and New York: Paulist Press).

Peter J. McCord, ed., *A Pope for All Christians?* (New York: Paulist Press).

6. Scripture

"Till I come, attend to the public reading of Scripture, to preaching, to teaching" (1 Tim. 4:13). "All Scripture is inspired by God and profitable for teaching, for reproof, for correction and for training in righteousness, that the man of God may be complete, equipped for every good work" (2 Tim. 3:16-17). Roman Catholics and Lutherans both use a unique book, the Bible. Through 450 years of separation, we have both followed a series of Scripture lessons in our Sunday liturgies which were almost identical. Recent revisions in the lectionary have kept us together in our "public reading of Scripture." We continue to agree on the central role that Scripture plays in the Church.

We have not, however, always interpreted that role in exactly the same way. Lutherans have often proclaimed the slogan, "Sola Scriptura" (Scripture alone) in a conscious effort to emphasize the primacy of the Scripture over against what appeared to them as a Roman Catholic emphasis on Church tradition. Roman Catholics, on the other hand, have pointed to the fact that the Scriptures originated within the community of God's people, the Church. These differences have frequently degenerated into stereotypes. Lutherans said that Roman Catholics regarded the Bible as a "chained book" which they could not read without permission from a priest. Roman Catholics thought that Lutherans interpreted the Bible according to their own whims quite apart from the faith of the Church.

Today at least one new fact has impressed people on both sides: Scripture is becoming more visibly important in the life of the Roman Catholic Church. At Masses on Sundays and major feasts, three Scripture lessons are read in the vernacular; Bible study groups are

107

multiplying in many parishes; new Bible translations are being bought and read by millions of Roman Catholic people. Roman Catholic Bible scholars are as widely known as those affiliated with other denominations. Some even serve on faculties of seminaries associated with other churches. Some Lutherans may be surprised by this seemingly recent blossoming of interest in Scripture among Roman Catholics. Surprise or not, the intensity of interest and the serious study of Scripture within the Roman Catholic Church cannot fail to have a helpful "fall-out" among Lutherans and other Christians.

Therefore let's take a serious look at the place of Scripture in our respective communities. The national Lutheran/Roman Catholic dialogue group has not dealt with this as a separate topic. Nevertheless, a regard for Scripture stands behind their work, and two significant volumes (*Peter in the New Testament*, 1973, and *Mary in the New Testament*, 1978) have resulted from common biblical study sponsored by the national dialogue.

Scripture in the Lutheran Church

If you were able to find the "average Lutheran" and ask what the Lutheran Church teaches about Scripture, he might answer: "Well, we believe that the Bible is the word of God. Anything that isn't taught in the Bible can't be taught in the Church—or at least anything that runs against what the Bible teaches can't. I believe in Jesus as my Lord and Savior because the Bible tells me so." Such an answer would be as close as any to being accurate, but in reality the Lutheran Church has no single official, or confessional, teaching about Scripture. The Augsburg Confession does not devote special attention to it, and neither do the other Lutheran confessional writings. The Epitome (or summary) of the Formula of Concord says very briefly: "We believe, teach, and confess that the prophetic and apostolic writings of the Old and New Testaments are the only rule and norm according to which all doctrines and teachers alike must be appraised and judged." This thought is repeated at a number of points throughout the Formula. What it says is that the canonical writings used in the Church are the source for all true teaching. It does not say, however, which writings these are or how they are to be interpreted.

This so-called "silence" of the Lutheran Confessions has led some to conclude that, for confessional Lutheranism at least, the question of Scripture in the Church is open-ended. Not only is there no list of those books of the Old and New Testaments that are considered canonical or official, but also the method by which one determines how Scripture is the "rule and norm" remains unsettled. Does this mean, then, that Lutherans do whatever they want with Scripture, or can we find within the Augsburg Confession itself a direction and a sense of the use of God's word, based itself upon a confessional principle?

Before we plunge into our search for answers to these questions, it might be helpful both for Lutherans and Roman Catholics to recall briefly the impact of Luther on the teachings articulated in the Augsburg Confession. The theological and life-oriented experience of this man—Augustinian friar, priest, teacher and doctor of Scripture, pastor of souls, dynamic personality—obviously has given the Lutheran Church a certain shape and distinct flavor quite beyond the mere borrowing of a name. Luther's personal search was for a God who justified—who accepted unconditionally—human beings without anything prior on their part which would merit that justification. The concise expression which Lutherans usually employ to say what Luther rediscovered in Scripture is that we are "justified by grace through faith."

In the Augsburg Confession, accordingly, faith is one thing only: trusting in Jesus Christ alone for salvation. Justification means that God gives us a new start in life in and through the Son Jesus Christ. God loves everyone not because we are good but because God is good—and God is good *for us* in the love revealed in the death and resurrection of Jesus Christ. God alone determines our future. This is the central teaching of the Augsburg Confession for those Christians within the Catholic Church now called "Lutherans." "Justification by grace through faith" is the cornerstone of Christian theology, the teaching by which the Church "stands or falls." It claims to be nothing less than a "spelling out" of Scripture, an "uncovering" of the heart of the Bible. All teachings, even of the Creeds or Scripture itself, are to be understood and interpreted with "justification by grace through faith" in mind.

Christ in the Scriptures

Of course, this does not mean that if someone says he believes this doctrine to be central, he necessarily is gifted by God to interpret correctly all Scripture for the Church. What it does mean for Lutherans, though, is that the Church is not bound to any one method or any one interpretation of Scripture. Lutherans believe that the Scripture is the word of God: "The Lutheran Reformation asserted unqualified dependence upon the prophetic and apostolic Scripture as the sole rule and standard by which all teachers and all teachings are to be judged and evaluated" (A. C. Piepkorn, *Profiles In Belief*, Volume II, p. 43). No individual, no theological school, no method can be promoted as *the* sole means by which the Church is to be instructed in the will of God; only Scripture can have that role—and Scripture understood as revealing to us God's unconditional acceptance of every person for the sake of Jesus.

This focus upon Scripture does not mean, however, that Lutherans are biblicists. They do not believe *in* the Bible. It is not the Bible that rules the Church; it is Christ and his word, in that order. It is Christ ruling through the word. That word is given in two forms. Scripture contains the law (what God commands us to do unconditionally) and the Gospel (the good news that God loves all persons for the sake of his Son without any prior merit of their own). The law functions primarily as the means that God uses to lead the unbeliever to see how far short of God's righteousness he has fallen through sin. Then, when one realizes the distance that separates human beings from God, the Gospel shines through as our only hope. It is not the law that is central in the life of the Church, but the Gospel; for in the Gospel God's love is made known through the atoning, sacrificial and victorious work of Jesus Christ. If Scripture in the life of the Church does not function in such a way as finally to lead us to faith in Jesus Christ, to believing the Gospel, then the Scripture is being used wrongly.

Although Lutherans believe that Scripture is the word of God, they do not equate the two. From a Lutheran perspective, Scripture is the word of God; the word of God, however, is more than written Scripture. Lutherans are bound, devoted, committed to Scripture, because through it God reveals *the* Word, Jesus Christ. This makes

Scripture as much a "means of grace" or a sacrament as baptism or the Eucharist. That is to say, through something earthly—human speech—God conveys to the believer his grace, love, forgiveness and eternal life. From the perspective of faith, Scripture is one of several means by which God reveals and manifests his love.

Lutherans and Scripture Today

All Lutherans are committed to the Augsburg Confession as a true explanation of Scripture. Not all Lutherans agree in their interpretation of Scripture. In fact, they are sometimes separated from one another within the Lutheran family precisely over the function of Scripture. Much ink and many words have flowed during the past 450 years with regard to the one area of the Church's life that the Confessions appear to have overlooked. Neither Luther nor the Confessions showed any great interest in explaining how, for instance, Scripture is the word of God. They were more concerned that Scripture should function as the word of God.

When, however, Lutherans started asking "How is it the word of God, and how then is it true?" they became embroiled in the gray area of theories regarding the inspiration, inerrancy, canonicity and infallibility of the Bible. Much of this discussion resulted from a neoscholasticism that some Lutheran theologians felt obligated to adopt in face of controversies that arose during the Counter-Reformation and, later on, during the Enlightenment. The need to define, to restrict, to codify an otherwise existential, confessing movement in the Church led to a certain rigidity of spirit in Lutheran biblical approaches.

We are beginning to see that this formalizing tendency was foreign to the spirit of Lutheranism as evidenced in the Augsburg Confession. We might compare it to the reluctance of the Confession and later Lutheranism to make an exclusive definition of "how" the Lord's body and blood are present in Holy Communion. Lutherans did not want to employ the medieval doctrine of transubstantiation; instead they were content to confess that the Lord's body and blood are truly present in Holy Communion for all to receive. Curiously, some of them later adopted a theory of divine inspiration that had God dictating the Bible word-for-word. The logical outcome of such efforts was the demand made by some Lutherans that all should believe, teach, and confess that Scripture is without any error in all matters—not only matters of faith, but also those of history, geography and the natural sciences. It should be noted, however, that this is the position of only a minority of contemporary Lutherans.

In fairness we should remember that other Christian communities have also passed through one or more of these stages of struggle in interpreting Scripture. Thus it is not surprising that many Lutherans have, until only recently, shared with others a rather simple view of the "truth" of Scripture. Often they were content to affirm a syllogism that stated: "God never lies or makes a mistake; the Holy Bible is the word of God; therefore, there are no mistakes or untruths in the Bible." However, that simple assumption has come under heavy attack.

The wide acceptance and use of the "higher critical method" in biblical studies came at a time when critics were attacking not only Scripture, but also many fundamentals of Christian faith itself. Some Lutherans saw the use of that method of understanding the Bible as a frontal attack on the foundation of the Church. There were, to be sure, a few who tried to use the higher critical method as a means to demolish or discredit the faith of Christians in the truthfulness of Scripture. The reaction of some Lutherans was defensiveness and fear; they found in other Christian communities what they thought was a handy weapon to be used against the enemy. That weapon was a theory of scriptural inerrancy or faultlessness that was foreign to the spirit of the Lutheran Confessions. While the Gospel must certainly be defended when attacked, it must first be proclaimed and celebrated. A study of the various literary forms which may be present in Scripture, and an understanding of how these relate to the formation of the scriptural tradition, does not imply or demand a loss of faith in the power of the Bible as the word of God for salvation. The Confessions teach that Scripture is the word of God not because it is inerrant or infallible, but because it is a revelation of Christ which is unique, as no other writings are or ever will be. Scripture has authority in the Church for Lutherans because it communicates the good news in a way comparable only to that of the sacraments.

What authority does Scripture have for Lutherans if it is the "only rule and norm"? Warren Quanbeck's summary statement from the first book of the Lutheran-Roman Catholic dialogues is instructive:

> *The Scriptures.* It is the word of God which calls the Church into being, maintains and preserves her, and the Church lives in loyalty and obedience to this word. The prophetic and apostolic witness to Jesus Christ the Word of God is found in the Scriptures, which for this reason have a primary place in the Church. *The authority of Scripture is the authority of the word of God, that is, the authority of the God who speaks in and through them.* This authority must not be understood in a literalistic, legalistic, or atomistic way, but is to be seen in the light of three factors *(Lutherans and Roman Catholics in Dialogue,* Volume I, p. 6; emphasis added).

The three factors to which Quanbeck refers are the Holy Spirit, the ministry and the problem of interpreting the Scriptures. The Holy Spirit works to permit us to hear God's voice today speaking through the Bible in the Church. It is the gift of the ministry through which God provides the living proclamation of the Gospel. The problem of interpretation points to the task of opening the literary, historical and theological dimensions of Scripture through knowledge of lexical, literary and historical information which help us better to understand the meaning of the text today. "The Bible is a record of the saving deeds of God, an interpretation of the significance of those deeds, and also an instrument through which God speaks in the life of the Church today," Dr. Quanbeck asserts.

The Use of Scripture in the Lutheran Community

Depending on what part of the Lutheran community you are examining as well as their specific purpose for being together, you are likely to find variety in the use of Scripture. Seminarians, participants in a Bible study group or Sunday school teachers would all use Scripture, but in ways that are externally quite different. They would all finally arrive at a common shared use: Scripture in the liturgy, in the worship of the Church. The Church of the Augsburg Confession (to use a more accurate description for "Lutherans") received its distinctive character largely through the liturgical preaching of the Gospel. The degree to which that preaching was at odds with the accepted theological ideas of the sixteenth century helped to produce points of disagreement between "Lutherans" and the Church of Rome. One of the two pillars supporting the true unity of the Church is the Gospel "preached in conformity with a true understanding of it" (Augsburg Confession, Art. VII). True unity is not based on agreement between exegetes about the tools used to interpret Scripture, but on preaching, proclaiming, and speaking the word of promise that leads to conversion and salvation. All study of Scripture, wherever and by whomsoever, must lead finally to its proclamation, or else such study is nothing more than an exercise in literary criticism.

Since Luther's revision of the medieval Mass in 1523 and 1526 (the *Formula Missae* and the German Mass), reading and preaching the word of God have been important elements in the liturgy of Lutheran churches. Although Holy Communion frequently suffered separation from the service of the Word, the proclamation of the Word was seldom omitted from the Eucharist. Lutherans in North America are rediscovering the unity of word and sacrament in their worship, the inseparable link between the two. Infrequent celebrations of Holy Communion (and the frequently-used service of "antecommunion") grew from a rationalistic understanding of the Gospel in which preaching was regarded more as edification and education than as proclamation.

The *Lutheran Book of Worship,* with its three-year lectionary based on the Roman Catholic one, clarifies the necessity to unite the liturgy of the Word with the liturgy of the Eucharist. In its directions to clergy and others responsible for worship, the *Lutheran Book of Worship* (Ministers' Edition) asserts: "Only under extraordinary circumstances would the sermon be omitted from this service (Holy Communion)" (p. 27). The notes also point out:

> Holy Communion has two principal parts. One centers in proclamation of the Word through the reading of the Scriptures and preaching; the other centers in sharing the sacramental meal. Surrounded by prayer, praise, and thanksgiving, these two parts

are so intimately connected as to form one unified act of worship. The Augsburg Confession regards Holy Communion as the chief act of worship on Sundays and other festivals (Article 24) (p. 25).

Lutherans, in common with other Christians, study Scripture privately and in small family gatherings, pray through the Scriptures by using psalms and biblical canticles, find consolation in God's word in time of need or trouble, sing and rejoice in the words of the Blessed Virgin Mary at Evening Prayer, and cry out in thankful hope with Zechariah at Morning Prayer. They teach their children to "read, mark, and inwardly digest" the word of God. They place it in the hands of their godchildren and all for whom they have a spiritual responsibility. The newly-ordained receive a copy of the Bible at their ordination with the words: "Receive these Holy Scriptures as a sign and token of your calling to preach and teach the word of God faithfully, governing life and doctrine by the apostolic and prophetic word" (*Proposed Rite of Ordination,* Inter-Lutheran Commission on Worship, 1977). Pastors and teachers promise to "preach and teach in accordance with the Holy Scriptures" and the Church's Confessions. The list could go on, but it would only further illustrate the commonality that Lutherans and Roman Catholics share in this area. The renewed faithfulness to Scripture and its wider use in public worship as well as in personal devotion are two of the most important areas of convergence among Lutherans and Roman Catholics today.

The Roman Catholic Church and Scripture

It might be tempting to remark that somehow Roman Catholics have "more" to say about the place of divine revelation in the Church, simply because their ecumenical councils have issued several important documents relating to revelation. The Councils of Florence and Trent, as well as the two Councils of the Vatican, provide in one form or another, definitive teachings for Roman Catholics regarding divine revelation in the life of the Church. Although such councils have spoken definitively about Scripture and revelation, this does not mean that all matters relating to them have been decided for all time. For instance, the First Vatican Council declared:

> The Church regards them (the various books of Scripture) as sacred and canonical . . . because, having been written under the influence of the Holy Spirit, they have God as their author and as such have been entrusted to the Church.

Regarding this declaration, the *Jerome Biblical Commentary* adds: "In the Catholic view, the divine inspiration of Scripture is, in the strict sense, a supernatural mystery. It is, therefore, a reality that can never be fully comprehended and that will always remain obscure and opaque to the human mind" (p. 500, paragraph 66:3). To this we might add: "And thus it will always be subject to the attempts of devout Christians to understand Scripture, revelation, and inspiration."

Lutherans have not failed to notice the exciting flowering of biblical studies within the Roman Catholic Church in this century. Less and less can other clergy disparagingly refer to their Roman Catholic brothers in the Ministry of word and sacrament as being mere "Mass priests" who rarely preach or, when they do, preach badly. Homiletics (the science of preaching), hermeneutics (the science of interpreting the word of God), and linguistics (the science of languages such as Greek, Aramaic and Hebrew) are the necessary tools for an intensive use of the Bible. These subjects are receiving increased emphasis in the curriculum of Roman Catholic seminaries. The mood in the Roman Catholic Church today is visibly encouraging a greater familiarity with the word of God among members of that Church.

Roman Catholic interest in the Bible has certainly not been confined to the last few years. Much has happened throughout the centuries to highlight the place of Sacred Scripture in the life of that Church. The world of biblical studies did not come to a speedy halt when St. Jerome's work ended in the early fifth century. What was true of biblical studies and theories in the Lutheran Church prior to the twentieth century was true, to a large degree, also of the Roman Catholic Church. For instance, until this century, most Roman Catholic scholars dated the composition of the books of the Bible as conservatively as did other Christian scholars. They affirmed, by and large, that any book of the Bible ascribed to a certain author was in fact written by that person. Both inspiration and inerrancy were defined in what we would today call a rather "fundamentalistic" or "literalistic" way. The view of inspiration which held sway was a theory of "dictation," one which found its authoritative beginnings in the Renaissance and Reformation, although it certainly had roots in some early Church Fathers.

For Roman Catholics, the Council of Florence (1442) decreed that those books then present in the Bible and acknowledged as commonly received were indeed canonical and authoritative for the Church. Thus not only did the Roman Catholic Church accept the Hebrew canon which is familiar to most Protestants, but it also accepted the deutero-canonical books (apocrypha) as part of the canon. Lutherans, on the other hand, have never formally defined the canon of Scripture, although by habit and usage only the Hebrew canon is commonly received (the books of the New Testament are the same for both communities).

A New Opening to Scripture

From the time of the First Vatican Council until the beginning of World War II, the Roman Catholic Church was busily engaged not only in dealing with the progress of scriptural studies in the Church but also in encountering the vigorous flowering of non-Catholic biblical criticism. Pope Leo XIII (see *Providentissimus Deus*) had to battle against both the Modernists within the Church and critics outside it. For this reason the Church of his time and thereafter had to leave to the side for the time being some of the more acceptable and helpful aspects of contemporary biblical studies. The charter of freedom for contemporary Roman Catholic biblical studies was the encyclical letter of Pope Pius XII, *Divino Afflante Spiritu* ("On the Promotion of Biblical Studies," 30 September 1945). Pius XII recognized the great change in thinking that had taken place in biblical studies during the past half century. Though remaining faithful in principle to the teachings of previous councils and to the principles laid down by his predecessors, he gave the Church's nod to biblical studies based on original texts. He allowed the use of textual criticism ("lower criticism"), opened the way for the use of "higher critical method" by encouraging the study of literary forms in the sacred books, and especially promoted the study and reading of Scripture by lay people.

Even though the way was difficult for Roman Catholic biblical scholars prior to 1945 partly because of the earlier Modernist controversy, there were many scholars who persevered. The wisdom of the Pontifical Biblical Commission in limiting itself to answering questions only in a limited fashion helped keep alive the serious pursuit of those areas of inquiry that were finally celebrated in the encyclical of Pius XII. Today, one of the outstanding and most popular products of Roman Catholic biblical studies is the *Jerome Biblical Commentary*. Its topical articles on everything from inspiration to eschatology are an invaluable resource for Roman Catholics and others, and the commentary is certainly a source of pride for the Church at large. This commentary, as well as the professional journals edited by Roman Catholic biblical scholars, truly illustrates the hope expressed by Pius XII when he wrote:

Nevertheless no one will be surprised if all difficulties are not yet solved and overcome; but even today serious problems greatly exercise the minds of Catholic exegetes. We should not lose courage on this account; nor should we forget that in the human sciences the same happens as in the natural world; that is to say, new beginnings grow little by little, and fruits are gathered only after many labors. . . . There are grounds for hope that those also will by constant effort be at last made clear, which now seem most complicated and difficult (*Divino Afflante Spiritu,* II, 44).

The hard questions to which Pius XII referred in 1945 are still with us in many ways: "In what way is Scripture to be understood as the word of God?" "What do we mean when we say: 'Word of God'?" "How can we speak of inspiration of Sacred Scripture, inerrancy, infallibility of the Word?" Although the Roman Catholic Church has, by and large, abandoned its former teaching about the direct verbal inspiration of Scripture, this does not mean that the Church has thrown inspiration out of the windows that were opened in 1945. It would be more correct to say that the inspiration of Sa-

cred Scripture is now taken to mean that Scripture lies under a positive divine influence. "One position sees inspiration as the divine
illumination of the practical judgment of the inspired writer, compil-
er, or editor so that he is able to choose the form and style that will
best suit his purpose. Other theologians see inspiration as a charismatic gift that the apostolic Church possessed, but that it was not
able to bequeath to later generations of Christians. There is a current
tendency to emphasize the social character of inspiration as the necessary consequence of the social character of literary composition in
the biblical period" (*Profiles in Belief,* I, p. 219).

Roman Catholics are usually less inclined than some Lutherans
to see inerrancy and the infallibility of Scripture in absolute terms.
They would more likely affirm that what is meant by the statement
"The Bible is true" is that the words of the Bible are regarded as true
"in the sense that the human writer conveys them within the patterns and forms of his own speech." This means, of course, that it
may be possible to see mistakes and errors of fact in the biblical writings, even contraditions of fact, but that there was no intent on the
part of the divine writer(s) to delude or lead us astray.

Revelation and Tradition

A point of difficulty arises when Lutherans and Roman Catholics speak about the place of tradition (often called "human" tradition) in the life of the Church. Often it has seemed to Lutherans that
Roman Catholics would like to place any and all traditions on an
equal level with revealed and written Scripture. Roman Catholics, on
the other hand, consider the Lutheran attitude toward tradition as
somewhat cavalier in its disregard for the historical deposit of faith
within the living experience of God's people. Lutherans, it appears,
seem to be trying to recreate a pristine, even simplistic understanding
of Scripture with little or no regard to the use which Scripture has
within the community and the community's tradition-filled life.

We must admit that the so-called "two-source theory" of divine
revelation (that is, Scripture and tradition on a complementary and
equal level) has been strong within the Roman Catholic Church, especially in this century. The first draft of the document submitted to
the Second Vatican Council concerning divine revelation was enti-

tled *On the Two Sources of Revelation*. The final product of the Council showed that the mind of the Church did not support a "two-source theory", and this we can see in the *Dogmatic Constitution on Divine Revelation* promulgated on 18 November 1965. This document does not solve all difficulties surrounding Scripture and tradition, but it does go far in helping both Roman Catholics and Lutherans come to a clearer understanding of Scripture, revelation and tradition—all within the context of the Church. While the document is too long to summarize here in any detail, it would be good to look at its view of Scripture and tradition by providing a few selected quotes.

The document emphasizes, first of all, the communication of God with humanity and especially with the community of persons called the Church (including Israel). This divine revelation to a community is important if we are to understand why tradition is essential and how it functions positively for Roman Catholics. Sacred tradition "and the sacred Scripture of both Testaments are like a mirror in which the Church, during her pilgrim journey here on earth, contemplates God, from whom she receives everything, until such time as she is brought to see him face to face as he really is (cf. Jn.3:2)" (*Dei Verbum* II, 7).

Tradition is another way of saying "apostolic," because what the Church preaches, teaches and confesses must be in the line of that tradition which has been handed down from the apostles to the Christian community of the present age. An understanding and insight into the Bible comes from the preaching of those who have received a calling from God through the Holy Spirit to tell the story of salvation and to convert hearers from non-belief to faith. "Sacred tradition and Sacred Scripture, then, are bound closely together and communicate one with the other. For both of them, flowing out of the same divine wellspring, come together in some fashion to form one thing and move toward the same goal. Sacred Scripture is the speech of God as it is put down in writing under the breath of the Holy Spirit. And tradition transmits in its entirety the word of God which has been entrusted to the apostles by Christ the Lord and the Holy Spirit. . . . Thus it comes about that the Church does not draw her certainty about all revealed truths from the holy Scriptures alone. . . . Both Scripture and tradition must be accepted and honored with equal feelings of devotion and reverence" (*Dei Verbum*, II, 9).

If Lutherans have reacted negatively to tradition linked insepa-rably with Scripture, it is because they believe that tradition must serve Scripture. Yet as *Dei Verbum* puts it: "The task of giving an authentic interpretation of the word of God, whether in its written form or in the form of tradition, has been entrusted to the living teaching office of the Church alone. Its authority in this matter is ex-ercised in the name of Jesus Christ. *Yet this magisterium is not supe-rior to the word of God, but is its servant*. . . . Working together, each (sacred tradition, Sacred Scripture, and the teaching office of the Church) in its own way under the action of the one Holy Spirit, they all contribute effectively to the salvation of souls" (II, 10). The em-phasis has been added to point out how close Roman Catholic and Lutheran thinking is on this matter. The teaching office of the Church authentically interprets the word of God. However, the teaching office is never above the word, but always in its service.

We find in *Dei Verbum* a perceptible move from a traditional orientation toward the relationship between Scripture and tradition to a more vital, dynamic understanding of their roles. Genuine tradi-tion, as the Lutheran historian Jaroslav Pelikan has said, is the "liv-ing faith of the dead." In the same regard, the Roman Catholic scholar Louis Bouyer writes: "Christian truth, revealed truth, is not just any truth. It is truth revealed precisely to make us live, to make us live the life which God desires for us. . . . We should think of Holy Scripture, therefore, above all as the place where we find Chris-tian truth expressed . . . as determined by the requirements of the vi-tal intercourse, the personal relationships, which God wishes to establish between man and himself." (*The Meaning of Sacred Scrip-ture*, Notre Dame Press, 1958).

Obviously many questions still remain unsettled in the area of Scripture and tradition for both Roman Catholics and Lutherans. We need to explore further the means by which tradition is passed on through and within the Christian community. We should examine more carefully the role of the laity and clergy, other than bishops, in forming and shaping tradition. How, for instance, do schools, semi-naries, religious communities, preaching, and private and public de-votions work together to shape tradition? What might we learn from a careful examination of tradition in the life of other Christian communities—for example, the Eastern Orthodox? What effect do languages, specific cultures and history itself have upon tradition? How do we approach traditions that seem, at least in part, to lack support in the early Fathers and thus seem to be without those roots that are common to both the Roman Catholic and Lutheran communities?

Dialogue To Heal the Breach

The sad division in the Church at the time of the Reformation occurred, according to the Augsburg Confession, because there was disagreement about how to interpret the Gospel in the life of the Church. Those who were called Lutherans championed "justification by grace through faith" as the key to their understanding of the word of God. They insisted that all Scripture should be interpreted with this teaching in mind.

Both Roman Catholics and Lutherans, using Scripture as their definitive source for the doctrines of the Church, have sometimes arrived at widely different interpretations of that one written deposit of revelation, or so it has seemed. Our willingness, through the prompting of God's Holy Spirit, to be in conversation with one another over such matters as baptism, the Eucharist, the Nicene Creed and the Church's Ministry has led us all finally back to that word of God. In returning to the common source, we are discovering many things about ourselves. As Louis Bouyer says, "In Sacred Scripture the truths of faith are immediately directed toward actual life. It is by no means accidental that this is the way in which these truths were given their primary, fundamental and, so to speak, 'fontal' form, that to which we must always go back when we wish to return to sources" (*op. cit.,* p. 2). We see that the sixteenth century, too, was colored and touched by "tradition" to such a degree that we twentieth-century Christians must devote ourselves to the task of re-examining both the causes of our division and the possibilities for our visible unity.

Lutherans call for the true unity of the Church with the deceptively simple formula "that the Gospel be preached in conformity with a pure understanding of it and that the sacraments be administered in accordance with the divine word" (Augsburg Confession,

Art. VII). The good news for our age, as one Lutheran commentator has noted, is that the bishops of the Roman Catholic Church no longer hinder the preaching of the Gospel in their churches (cf. Apology of the Augsburg Confession, Art. XIV, 5). St. Jerome, in commenting on the prophet Isaiah, once wrote: "Ignorance of the Scriptures is ignorance of Christ" (*Commentary on Isaiah,* Prologue). Such knowledge comes not just from apologetics or dialectics, but is first and foremost the knowledge that is gained through communion with Christ in worship. "Let them remember, however, that prayer should accompany the reading of Sacred Scripture, so that a dialogue takes place between God and man. For, 'we speak to him when we pray; we listen to him when we read the divine oracles' " (*Dei Verbum,* VI, 25, quoting St. Ambrose).

This brings us, finally, to something to which we have alluded above, namely, the sacramental nature of Scripture. There is, for both Roman Catholics and Lutherans, a powerful, close parallel to be drawn between the word and the sacraments. As the Second Vatican Council has taught, "The Church has always venerated the divine Scriptures as she venerates the body of the Lord insofar as she never ceases, particularly in the sacred liturgy, to partake of the bread of life and to offer it to the faithful from the table of the word of God and the body of Christ" (*Dei Verbum,* VI, 1). This Roman Catholic statement serves well as a summary for Lutherans, too.

FOR STUDY AND DISCUSSION

1. What is the Roman Catholic view of the "canon" of Scripture? How is it established and how many books are included? Compare this with the Lutheran view of the "canon" of Scripture.
2. What is the Lutheran evaluation of the books referred to as "apocrypha"?
3. This chapter speaks of the confession that "the Bible is the word of God." What is the relation of "word of God" to the Bible? How has the term "word of God" been used in Christian faith and theology? Is the word of God limited to the Bible?
4. What do Lutherans view as the central teaching of Scripture?
5. What are the two forms of the word contained in Scripture?
6. How is it possible to say that Scripture is a "means of grace"?

7. What theories of biblical inspiration are found among Lutherans? Among Roman Catholics?
8. What are the issues in the debates over the "higher critical" interpretation of Scripture?
9. What is the main function of Scripture according to the Lutheran confessions?
10. What, if any, is the distinction between "inerrancy" and "infallibility" with regard to the Bible?
11. How do Roman Catholics regard the relation between Scripture and tradition? How do Lutherans relate them?
12. Which came first, the Bible or the Church? Discuss all the ramifications of that much-discussed question.
13. People who have a high regard for Scripture sometimes arrive at different views concerning its teachings. How do Lutherans and Roman Catholics each deal with that paradox?
14. According to the Lutheran Confessions, what is necessary for the true unity of the Church? How would Roman Catholics react to that view of Church unity?

FOR FURTHER READING

Arthur C. Piepkorn, *Profiles in Belief,* Volumes I and II (New York: Harper and Row).

Austin Flannery, ed., *Documents of Vatican Council II* (Northport, N.Y.: Costello Publishing Co.).

Raymond Brown *et al.,* eds., *Mary in the New Testament* (Philadelphia: Fortress Press, and New York: Paulist Press).

Jean Daniélou, *The Bible and the Liturgy* (Ann Arbor, Mich.: Servant Books).

J. Lindblom, *The Bible—A Modern Understanding* (Philadelphia: Fortress Press).

Claus Westermann, *Handbook to the Old Testament* and *Handbook to the New Testament* (Minneapolis: Augsburg Publishing House).